CLEVELAND ROCKS:

A Bicentennial Political and Social History of Cleveland 1796 - 1996

DAMON STAKES

Cuyahoga Community College

YORK PUBLISHING COMPANY
CLEVELAND, OHIO

ISBN 0-9634940-4-X

Library of Congress Catalog Card Number: 94-61085

Printed in the United States of America

10 9 8 7 6 5 4 3 2 1

York Publishing Company
16781 Chagrin Blvd. #336
Shaker Heights, Ohio 44120
Phone: (216) 491-0231
Fax: (216) 491-0251
1995

Preface

Cleveland Rocks begins with a historical account of the men, women and events that molded Cleveland into a major metropolitan area. In the opening section the reader is briefly introduced to the city's often ignored native American heritage and then to the ethnic, racial and cultural mosaic that contributed to Cleveland's diverse social fabric. From the founding of Cleveland until 1962, the unique contributions of the city are blended into part of America's history in "A Concise History of Cleveland."

The rewards and consequences of Cleveland's mayoral decisions are portrayed in "Power Politics in Cleveland." Here Cleveland Rocks captures the essence of political developments from Ralph Locher to the present. Using some behind the scenes information, the book delves into the major movers, shakers, shapers and makers of public policy decisions in Cleveland.

Contemporary social issues and problems are presented in the third section of the work. Part III begins by returning to the multi-cultural diversity of this area and then expands into economic and social issues and problems of greater Cleveland, as it explores the relationships, the city, the county and the metropolitan area that encompasses the Census Bureau's Standard Metropolitan Statistical Area.

Although each section of Cleveland Rocks is written from a different vantage point, either historical, political, or from the perspective of a social scientist, they all blend into an objective appraisal of the political and social history of Cleveland.   Over twenty years of research and writing has been committed to this endeavor. This work localizes historical events, civil and equal rights struggles, multi-cultural diversity, political issues and social problems. Throughout the book, historical peculiarities, humor, and thought provoking insights tantalize or challenge the reader.

Part I ends with an annotated bibliography of suggested readings, while individual chapters are referenced with end notes at the conclusion of each chapter in Parts II and III. Please take note of the Suggestions for Further Reading and the References, at times the best has been saved for last.

As a former junk yard scavenger, cab and truck driver, student teacher and substitute for the Berea, Cleveland, Lakewood and Parma school systems, Ford Foundry worker, McDonald's server, office worker, mental health attendant, laborer, carpenter, electrician and house painter, and now as a world traveler, writer, Associate Professor of History and Political Science, and generally lost (males don't ask for directions) driver, I have experienced much that others may have avoided, ignored or missed about this community. Assuredly you are going to learn something new about Cleveland.

To All Clevelanders

Table of Contents

Tables

Maps

Graphics, Photography, Art/Design and Layout,
by Marie Stakes

PART I

A CONCISE HISTORY OF CLEVELAND

PRE-CLEAVELAND HISTORY

At precisely 9:37 A.M., on June 17, 9796 B.C., give or take a couple hundred years, Paleolithic hunters settled along the Cuyahoga River basin on Lake Erie's southern shore. Receding glaciers sculpted the Great Lakes into one fifth of the world's fresh water reserves, nurturing the growth of dense forests. This ecosystem in turn sustained fish and other aquatic creatures, a vast assortment of birds, and mammals from the shrew to elk, moose, antelope, buffalo, mountain lions, black bears, and timber wolves. These original inhabitants of Cleveland may have also encountered a number of extinct life forms like the stag moose, giant sloth or the saber cat whose remains have been discovered by archaeologists in neighboring Great Lake States.

Gradually these nomadic prehistoric transients were replaced by Neolithic Archaic Indians. These hunters, fishermen, and food–gathers gradually created a more sedentary stone–age culture that eventually evolved into a distinct Woodland tradition. Undoubtedly, the most evident and impressive achievements of the early Woodland Indians can be found in the earthworks and burial mounds that remain throughout Ohio. Archeological evidence indicates that Ohio's Mound Builders, the Hopewell, were part of an interwoven, complex and highly stratified society. They were deeply religious, venerating the dead, and since divergent construction and burial patterns existed, each Hopewell settlement remained semi–autonomous, similar to the city–states that characterized much of the ancient world.

Living in small hamlets near these burial centers each village specialized in providing a specific marketable commodity or dietary component to the whole. Roadways, the first discovered by the Ohio Historical Society in 1993, enabled goods and the necessary manpower needed to build the elaborate burial mounds to travel to their assigned destinations. The Hopewell developed a flourishing trade network, that extended from the Rocky Mountains to the Gulf of Mexico. Ultimately, this commercial relationship fostered a sophisticated lapidary industry enabling the Mound Builders to design intricate copper and stone jewelry, musical instruments and figurines.

Sometime prior to 1000 A.D., the Hopewell ceased constructing the mounds that had characterized their society. A change in climate probably caused the Mound Builders to abandon a way of life that had lasted for centuries. Ancient civilizations were tremendously dependent upon weather conditions for their survival, without adequate storage or curing techniques, any prolonged change in climate could doom the existence of any early culture.

Although the principal mounds in Cleveland have vanished, two of the city's major thoroughfares continue to venerate the Hopewell. Unbeknownst to most Clevelanders, East 9th Street and Euclid Avenue once served as a Hopewell burial mound which encouraged surveyors to choose it as a major bisecting route. Cleveland remains part of a ten thousand year native American heritage that extends beyond the Indian word for "crooked," Cuyahoga, that denotes the City's principal river and county.

By the mid–seventeenth century, when the French began mapping and exploring the Great Lakes, they found the eastern part of Lake Erie inhabited by the powerful Cat Nation, the Erie Indians. Lake Erie is named for these hunters of the raccoon, which the French deemed the wildcat. The Erie Indian's blankets and robes were made from the pelts and fringed with the ringed tails of the raccoon. The principal domain of the Cat People extended from Niagara Falls to the Cuyahoga River basin.

Seeking allies in her quest to dominate the North American fur trade, the French intensified long seated rivalries between the Erie and her traditional enemy, the Iroquois. According to the earliest historical account of this area, *Jesuit Relations*, the Iroquois Confederation sought to become the preeminent power in the Eastern Great Lakes. In an imperialistic attempt to become the North American middleman for the Great Lakes fur trade, the Iroquois defeated the former French pelt suppliers: the Huron, the Tionotate (Tobacco Nation), and the Attiwandaron (Neutral Nation), between 1649 and 1651. The only obstacle remaining for the Iroquois was the destruction of the Cat Nation, whose hunting prowess had long been well established.

The Iroquois or Beaver Wars succeeded in cutting off much of the French supply of fur pelts. Once economically vulnerable, the French were easily beguiled by the Iroquois offer of alliance and their supposed willingness to accept religious conversion. With Machiavellian mastery of *realpolitik*, the Iroquois had previously secured flintlocks from the Dutch and the English. Having duped the French into providing even more weapons, the Iroquois Confederation launched their assault on the Erie in 1654, within two years the Cat Nation was totally obliterated. When Casson, Galinee, Jolliet and Pere explored the southern shores of Lake Erie in 1669, the Erie were gone and their villages destroyed.

3

The annihilation of the hunters of the wildcat ultimately opened this region to a variety of Indian tribes.

The major nations that lived within Ohio's borders included the Delaware, Miami, Ottawa, Shawnee, and Wyandot. Prior to the Revolutionary War, these Indian tribes lived a semi–sedentary life-style without territorial boundaries and in relative tranquillity, unless harassed from outsiders. The few examples of conflicts among these tribes were actually provoked by European traders, settlers, or soldiers, who encouraged the Indians to wage war upon one another or upon vulnerable frontiersmen.

Although the French were forced out of North America by the Treaty of Paris 1763, her Indian allies, united by the Ottawa Chief, Pontiac, managed to temporarily terminate colonial migration beyond the Appalachian Mountains. Furthermore, the British imposed the Proclamation Line of 1763, which forbade any settlement beyond the Appalachians by the colonists. For one final decade, Ohio remained under the control of the Woodland Indians. Their hold was shattered by the opening shots of the American Revolutionary War in the fall of 1774.

The American Revolutionary War actually began in Ohio. The opening battle for American independence was not fought at Lexington or Concord, but at Point Pleasant, Ohio, on October 10, 1774. Furthermore, America's first Declaration of Independence was originally proclaimed in Ohio's Fort Gower Resolves on November 5, 1774, not in Philadelphia on July 4, 1776.

Ohio's involvement in the American Revolutionary War and perhaps the Revolutionary War itself centered around John Murray the 4th Earl of Dunmore. Lord Dunmore was a Scottish born peer, a position that enabled him to become the British Governor of New York in 1770. But the following year he was asked to become Governor of Virginia, a job that Dunmore did not quite relish Upon hearing of the appointment, he was said to have become too cheerful in drinking and ran through the streets, striking passerby's, and shouting: "Damn Virginia! I asked for New York and they give me Virginia."

Despite his initial disappointment, Dunmore blended in well with the Virginia aristocracy. His leadership was a combination of flamboyance, authoritarianism, and greed; the colony became his personal domain. His authoritarian temper offered little sympathy or understanding for the Virginia aspirations for autonomy. He twice dissolved the Virginia House of Burgesses when they supported actions challenging British rule. But Lord Dunmore shared one important characteristic with Virginians – a hunger for land. In violation of the Proclamation Line of 1763, he participated in western land speculation, Virginia's original sea-to-sea grant enabled her to claim the present states of Kentucky, West Virginia, Ohio, Indiana, Illinois, Michigan and Wisconsin. This common interest in land was to bind men like George Washington and other members of the Virginia aristocracy to their new governor's ambition to open the Ohio River area for settlement. Dunmore's order to the Virginia militia to seize the upper Ohio River changed the destiny of an empire and inspired the colonial quest for independence.

Until the incursions by Dunmore, the frontier (Ohio) was quiet. Fort Pitt, the only major settlement beyond the Appalachians, had been abandoned. The Indians did not feel threatened, and as long as the Proclamation Line remained enforced, the Indians lived in relative tranquillity. On January 1, 1774, a Virginia militia entered the abandoned Fort Pitt claiming it for Virginia, renaming it Fort Dunmore and prepared for an Indian counterattack. However, reckless frontiersmen, under Captain Michael Cresap, struck first, attacking the Mingo Indians encamped on Yellow Creek above Steubenville, murdering the sister and brother of the Mingo Chief Logan, a friend of the white settlers. A second expedition from Wheeling crossed the Ohio entering Indian territory, and moved near present–day Coshocton.

On September 30, 1774, Lord Dunmore personally commanded a force of 1200 men that moved from Wheeling, to Fort Dunmore, to Fort Gower and then into the heart of Shawnee territory, Camp Charlotte. Meanwhile, a second force led by Colonel Andrew Lewis moved to Point Pleasant on the Ohio River. On October 10, 1774, Lewis met a force of a thousand Delaware, Shawnee, Mingo and Ottawa warriors led by Cornstalk, the able Shawnee Chief. Although the Indians fought bravely they were forced to retreat with heavy losses. Caught in this pincer movement, the Indians were forced to sign the Treaty of Camp Charlotte which guaranteed unmolested travel along the Ohio River.

Upon returning to Fort Gower from the Camp Charlotte meeting, Lord Dunmore's officers drew up a series of resolves that present the basic colonial argument for independence. On Guy Fawkes Day, November 5, 1774, six months before Lexington, the Fort Gower Resolves were adopted by Dunmore's commanders:

Resolved that we will bare the most careful allegiance to His Majesty King George III, whilst his Majesty reigns over a brave and free people.

And that we will at the expense of life and of everything dear and valuable assert ourselves in support of his crown and the British Empire.

We resolve that we will exert every power within us for the defense of American liberty, and for the support of her just rights and privileges, but not in a precipitous or riotous manner when regularly called forth by the unanimous voice of our countrymen.

We entertain the greatest respect for the honorable Lord of Dunmore who commanded the expedition in the Shawnee conflict. (His motives were in the) true interest of this country.

The Fort Gower Resolves represent the first colonial statement differentiating American and English liberty. Note that the Resolves refer to a distinct "brave and free people," with a separate designation for "American liberty." Further, the final Resolve recognizes the existence of a separate colonial entity when it refers to "this country" when referring to American interests. In actuality the Fort Gower Resolves can be considered the first "Declaration of Independence." Moreover, the Fort Gower Resolves were republished by all the colonies that had western land claims beyond the Appalachians. Through the Virginia *Gazette*, Pennsylvania *Gazette*, Connecticut *Gazette*, and the Essex and Salem newspapers of Massachusetts, news of the Resolves were transmitted to other colonies, inspiring similar thoughts of independence elsewhere in the colonies.

When England sought to punish the colonists for the Boston Tea Rebellion, they attacked the western land claims in the northwest territory. In the Quebec Act, the British attempted to give the lands north of the Ohio River, opened by Lord Dunmore's War, over to the French speaking population. This threatened the western land claims, not only of Massachusetts, but those of Virginia, Pennsylvania, and Connecticut as well. It was the Quebec Act more than the actions taken solely against Massachusetts that convinced the colonists to join together to fight for their rights, western lands, liberties, and Ohio!

Lord Dunmore's War and the British acceptance of American Independence, the Treaty of Paris 1783, removed the two greatest obstacles to frontier settlement, the Indian resistance and the English Proclamation Line. Squatters and speculators were already active before the Continental Congress adopted the Land Ordinance of 1785. The Land Ordinance authorized a survey of the new territories given to the Articles by member states willing to relinquish control of western lands beyond the Appalachians in lieu of Revolutionary War debts. This would lead to the last major success of the Articles, the Northwest Ordinance of 1787. Written by Thomas Jefferson, the Northwest Ordinance banned slavery, provided for public education (allocating a portion of all land revenues to be committed to education) and established county governments, territorial assembles, and finally a binding commitment to statehood for what would become Ohio, Indiana, Illinois, Michigan, and Wisconsin.

Connecticut a perennial loser in the overlapping land claims, lost Long Island to New York under the British, and then a U.S. Federal Court ruling deprived her claim to northern Pennsylvania in 1782. In 1786, Connecticut conceded the bulk of her western lands to the first government of the United States, the Articles of Confederation, though she retained a western reserve. This approximately 1.2 million acres was reserved to Connecticut as compensation for her earlier losses. Ultimately, Connecticut's Western Reserve would be incorporated by the governor of the Northwest Territory, Arthur St. Clair, into the Ohio Territory. During the interim 1786 to 1800, the Connecticut Land Company purchased the bulk of the Western Reserve envisioning the establishment of New Connecticut, to this end, the company sent a surveying party into the lands of the Western Reserve.

THE LONG CHAPTER (1796-1900)

After wandering in the wilderness, in what may have seemed like years, Moses founded Cleveland. Some three thousand years after emerging from...wait!

Cleveland was founded by a true Connecticut Yankee, Moses Cleaveland. He was a strong-willed Yale graduate, a lawyer, a member of the Connecticut legislature and a recently commissioned Brigadier General in the state's militia. As the official representative of the Connecticut Land Company, which he helped form and on whose board of directors he served, Cleaveland was to secure the land from the Indians, survey the purchase, and establish a capital for the future state of New Connecticut.

Joseph Hodge, an African American frontiersmen and fur trapper, was engaged by Cleaveland to serve as guide and Indian interpreter. Hodge led the 50 man expedition into the uncharted wilderness and helped negotiate the purchase of the Western Reserve, from the Six Iroquois Nations at a meeting near Buffalo Creek. The Mohawk and Seneca representatives of the Six Nations accepted 500 pounds of New York currency, two beef cattle, and 100 gallons of whiskey for the lands from the crooked water, Cuyahoga River, to the Pennsylvania border.

Cleaveland's surveying party entered the Western Reserve in time to observe the first Independence Day Celebration in the Reserve at Conneaut Creek, which they appropriately named Port Independence, thereby raising the concerns of the neighboring Massasagoes Indians. Subsequent negotiations with Chief Paqua allowed the surveying party to proceed in exchange for $25 worth of goods and whiskey. Soon afterwards, the General and a small band proceeded by boat along the Lake Erie shoreline to found the capital for New Connecticut. Arriving on July 22, 1796, Cleaveland's expedition reached its goal, the Cuyahoga River delta.

Cleaveland was not the first to journey into the uncharted frontier. At least one representative from the Northwest Fur Company had earlier constructed and abandoned a dwelling to benefit from the lucrative fur trade with the Ottawa, Delaware, and Chippewa tribesmen that resided in this area. However, the Connecticut Yankee was the first to view this site as a place of permanent settlement. By mid-October, the expedition had completed the survey of the Western Reserve and returned to Connecticut.

In 1796, Ohio was considered an untamed wilderness. Cleaveland's exploration and survey made inexpensive land available to those who had the desire and pioneering spirit to venture beyond the Appalachians into an uncertain future. In the eighteenth century, Ohio was teaming with elk, deer, moose, and even buffalo. There were very few major carnivorous predators like bears or wolves, other than man, to prey upon these majestic herbivores. Properly managed many of these native species could be returned to their original habitat in the Cuyahoga Valley National Recreational Area.

Cleveland's first permanent settler was Lorenzo Carter. Carter arrived with his brother-in-law and their families from Vermont in May 1797, and they constructed a large cabin which served as a hotel, restaurant, and tavern for travelers as well as a trading post for tribesmen. During the early years of the settlement, Lorenzo Carter served as a bonding agent to keep the small community together; he provided the spark. Carter was a man of vision and ingenuity, he served as the unofficial mayor, sheriff, and magistrate and his tavern even served as the local jail. In 1802, he constructed the first frame house in Cleveland, unfortunately this structure was destroyed by fire soon after completion. Later he built a block house that became the township's first true hotel which also served as the first school house. In 1808, Carter began Cleveland's shipbuilding tradition by building the *Zephyr* which was designed for lake trading. The *Zephyr* was a flat bottomed craft that sent Cleveland-made grindstones and furs to the east for dry goods, groceries, iron and salt. In the early nineteenth century, vinegar and salt were the main preservatives for vegetables and meat.

Im 1809, George Peake became the first permanent African American resident in greater Cleveland. At the age of eighty-seven, he arrived with his family, purchasing one hundred acres near the mouth of the Rocky River in Lakewood. He was the first wagon traveler and the first to follow the new Cleveland-Huron road, although I believe he was delayed an additional forty-five minutes until the orange barrels were removed. As the inventor of a grain milling device, George Peake was among the most respected and wealthiest residents of this area until his death at the age of one-hundred and five.

Cleveland's early history was very inauspicious. In 1800, the population reached seven, a decade later the hamlet zoomed up to fifty-seven and by 1820, Cleveland languished as a typical Great Lake and river town with a population of only 606. The largest North Coast settlements in Ohio were Ashtabula, population 929, and Huron, population 651. Two other noteworthy and commercial rivals were Lorain (Black River), population 354 and Sandusky, population 243.

Further settlement was temporarily thwarted by the emergence of the last great Woodland Indian confederation. Led by Chief Tecumseh and "the Prophet," a medicine man, these Shawnee brothers forged a vast Indian alliance from Michigan to Mississippi. Tecumseh provided the political leadership, traveling to various Indian encampments trying to gain their commitment to the alliance, while his brother provided spiritual inspiration. Upon one such journey, Tecumseh came upon a small tribe that he failed to win over. Finally, he threatened to destroy their homes and village by stamping his feet when he returned north to his Shawnee camp. Unimpressed, they still refused. A short time afterward, this village was leveled by the greatest earthquake to strike the central United States. The New Madrid quake in 1811 was so massive that for a time the Mississippi River actually flowed northward and the delta was permanently moved over fifty miles to its present location. They knew that Tecumseh had indeed fulfilled his promised revenge.

In November, 1811, William Henry Harrison's victory over the Prophet at Tippecanoe Creek, Indiana, became the catalyst for the "Second War for Independence." Alarmed by the mistaken belief that the British were behind the Indian unification efforts, Western and Southern Congressmen, claiming maritime trade restrictions and impressment, voted overwhelmingly for war against Britain. They hoped to gain control of the lucrative fur trade and acquire Canada and Spanish Florida. "The best laid plans of mice and men..." Not only did the United States fail in the attempt to gain any of these primary objectives, she had to also endure the burning of the new nation's Capital in Washington, DC. Unplanned, uncoordinated, and unsupported by many Americans, the war effort failed to accomplish it's goals. Early in the conflict even Detroit was lost to the British.

"We have met the enemy and they are ours," Captain Oliver Hazard Perry reported after defeating an inferior British naval force near Put-in-Bay, Ohio. This victory in September, 1813, gave the United States control over the Great Lakes and made the English hold over Detroit untenable, enabling Harrison to defeat Tecumseh in October. At Dunham Tavern on Euclid Avenue, a huge wall painting depicts the Battle of Lake Erie. Incidentally, a quarter of Perry's forces were made up of African Americans.

These military successes convinced the British to retaliate. Originally tied down with her conflict with Napoleon, the English could only send token resistance to the Americas, however with Napoleon in Elba, she turned her attention to ravaging the East Coast. Although British maritime forces burned the Capital, the White House and other public buildings in 1814, English ground forces were unable to capitalize upon their successful Chesapeake Bay naval raid. Because of the battlefield stalemate, Tsar Alexander convinced both sides to end the conflict with a permanent cease-fire and a demilitarization of the Great Lakes, when he helped to mediate the Treaty of Ghent.

Meanwhile in the southwest, Andrew Jackson followed up his victory over the Creeks at Horseshoe Bend by defeating the Spanish garrison at Pensacola. Finally, Jackson recorded Americas greatest victory during the War of 1812. This event actually took place two weeks after the Treaty of Ghent had been signed in Europe, when Jackson decisively defeated a superior British force at the Battle of New Orleans in January, 1815. The west was once again open for renewed settlement.

Although the victory over the Tecumseh's Woodland Indian confederation was complete, a volcanic eruption halfway around the globe would once again devastate the agrarian frontier for another year. Mount Tambora erupted in Indonesia in April, 1815, recording the greatest eruption by a volcano. The catastrophic impact of the largest volume of ash ever recorded (Guinness) in the atmosphere would dramatically affect the world's climates. This resulted in the coldest summer experienced in US. History. Continual crop failures would bring actual starvation to America's frontier during the "Year Without a Summer."

One day before the Treaty of Ghent was signed, "Cleveland," with her present spelling, was recognized as an incorporated village by the Ohio General Assembly. The legislature adopted the present spelling of Cleveland when the village was incorporated. She held her first municipal election in 1815, electing Alfred Kelley as president of the village.

Alfred Kelley's contribution to the early development of Cleveland was immense. He was Cleveland's first practicing attorney and the first prosecutor for Cuyahoga County. Elected to the state legislature in 1814, Kelley became the catalyst for the state recognizing village status for Cleveland, suggesting a population base well beyond the dynamics of the small community. More importantly, as an assemblyman on the canal commission, he secured Cleveland as northern terminus for the Ohio Canal.

Cleveland quickly felt the impact of the Ohio Canal. Completed in 1825, the Erie Canal (from New York City to Buffalo) had opened the East Coast to expanded commercial activities along the Great Lakes. Now the interior regions would be opened for Ohio commerce to both northern (Cleveland, east) and later southern (Cincinnati, south), markets. Canal laborers, builders and merchants transformed the village into a mini metropolis, with new warehouses, cargo, and workers striving to benefit from new trade and employment opportunities.

In many ways the Erie Canal severed Cleveland's ties to Connecticut. Settlers increasingly came from New York, rather than Connecticut or New England. Cleveland became more cosmopolitan both ethnically and philosophically. A noticeable number of German and Irish immigrants, originally attracted by the construction of the Ohio Canal, remained in the city. Also traveling along the muddy waters of the Erie Canal were the religious and social thoughts which would ultimately transform the northern concept of God.

The Old Testament and Calvinist concept of a God of wrath, accepting infant damnation, predestination, and slavery, was challenged. Northerners began to accept the New Testament and the Second Awakening's idea of a merciful and benevolent deity who recognized good works as a vehicle for eternal salvation. This inspired a reform movement which promoted an active concern for the less fortunate. Abolitionist and temperance societies appeared in Cleveland. By 1836, printers and carpenters had formed local unions and a public school system had been inaugurated for the city. Cleveland's Central High was the first public high school built west of the Alleghenies when founded in 1845. Ultimately, America's major churches divided over the concept of God and slavery, which set the stage for the most destructive conflict in America's History - the Civil War.

Population growth and ethnic diversity also altered the size and nature of Cleveland's religious organizations. By 1845, there were a dozen Protestant congregations, two exclusively German, one African American, a Roman Catholic Church, St. Mary's on the Flats, and two Jewish congregations in the city. By 1836, due to the influx of new inhabitants, Cleveland was officially recognized as a city by the State of Ohio. An additional indication of the ethnic transformation of Cleveland was evident by the publication of the first German language newspaper, *Germania*, in the city in 1846. A century and a half later, Cleveland still supports a half dozen ethnic newspapers.

Being tied to the national economy also had destructive consequences. The Panic of 1837 adversely affected the local economy and canal trade for over half a decade. The canal's traffic rebounded in the mid-Forties, reaching their heights in the early 1850's, just as they were being replaced by rail transportation.

Alfred Kelley and Cleveland would once again take the lead in financing, designing, manufacturing and building Ohio's first major railroad, the Cleveland, Columbus, and Cincinnati Railroad. Alfred Kelley was the president of Cleveland, Columbus, and Cincinnati Railroad. Ohio's first locomotive, *The Cleveland*, was built on the west bank of the Cuyahoga River in Ohio City.

Ohio City was once a political and commercial rival to Cleveland. She became a city two days before Cleveland and benefited from the traffic which flourished from the only bridge that crossed the Cuyahoga. An armed conflict arose when Cleveland built a second bridge, diverting trade from Ohio City. Although no injuries were recorded, antagonism remained until the twin cities voted to merge in 1854. Both cities decided that maintaining duplicate services unfairly punished their taxpaying citizens.

Today such logic escapes most suburban politicians. Although many suburbs have found it advantageous to consolidate their school systems, they still have separate mayors, councils, fire and police chiefs, law directors, recreational and service officials, ad-in-finitum. Individually they remain vulnerable to cable television, trash removal and utility companies that have already realized that operating united can be extremely profitable. Apparently, one hundred years later, Cleveland's suburbs continue to insist that Charles Darwin was wrong.

From Lake Erie, the Cuyahoga River, and the multitude of canals and railroads, came the raw materials and food stuffs necessary to sustain local inhabitants. However, typical of most pre-Civil War cities, few area goods were manufactured for export. The only Cleveland product that appeared to have a national audience was the publication in 1855, of Harriet Beecher Stowe's *Uncle Toms Cabin*. When President Abraham Lincoln later met the author, he said: "So you're the little women that wrote the book that made this Great War." OK, with a stretch, Cleveland started the Civil War, by publishing the most significant work in pre-Civil War US. History.

On the eve of the Civil War, Cleveland began to assume the appearance of a mature city. By the end of the 1850's, Cleveland became a major transportation center for the nation with five railroads operating from the Forest City. A tree planting movement during 1850 and 1851, established Cleveland as the Forest

City. Judiciously planted, mature trees currently enhance the value of a home anywhere from between two to five thousand dollars and protect the environment by replenishing the Earth's depleted oxygen supply. By 1860, Forest City could boast of a public education system educating 6,000 students, a permanent board of health, 10 fire engines with 500 volunteer fire-fighters, gas-lit downtown streets, a professional police force of 40 patrolmen, and a Federal District Court.

When Abraham Lincoln sought a force of 75,000 men nationwide to deal with secessionist conflict, Ohio alone volunteered 100,000. Both the North and the South were ready for war. America was truly a nation divided, divided socially, economically, religiously and politically with Lincoln's election. The Cleveland Grays, the local militia, enlisted in the 1st Ohio Volunteer Infantry. They were the first Union soldiers to enter the field of battle at Bull Run and the last to leave; the Grays remained loyal to their country with their motto *Semper Paratus* -"always ready," and they served nobly throughout the national crisis.

An unprepared peacetime economy was rapidly converted to meet military needs. Agricultural prices accelerated beyond wage increases, financial institutions failed, and manpower shortages were evident. Economic dislocation and the unforeseen length of conflict led the *Plain Dealer* to support Clement L. Vallandigham, the leader of the Peace Democrats, in his unsuccessful gubernatorial bid in 1863. Forced into Canada by Union forces, Vallandigham became known as "the man without a country." Later the leader of the Peace Democrats or "Copperheads" (worse than a rattlesnake) would unsuccessfully make a bid for the Presidency. Another interesting sidelight to this tumultuous era, John Wilks Booth performed his last professional engagement in Cleveland before joining the Confederates.

The Civil War became a catalyst for American industry. Wartime requirements necessitated manufacturing on an unprecedented scale. Following the war, these gigantic factories remained to forge a new future for the city. During the 1860's, Cleveland's population more than doubled, as heavy industry and manufacturing began to replace commercial enterprises. These economic changes fostered new employment opportunities which attracted immigrants from Southern and Eastern Europe, as large numbers of Croatians, Czechs, Greeks, Hungarians, Italians, Poles, Russian Jews, Serbs, Slovaks, and Slovenians made their way into the Forest City. By the end of the decade, over forty percent of the city's population were foreign born.

In 1868, America's first National Woman's Suffrage Con-

vention was held in Cleveland. Although this convention advocated granting voting rights to women, it was timid compared to
the Woman's Rights Convention held two decades earlier, in
Seneca Falls, New York. The Women's Rights Convention advocated equality between the sexes, unbelievably the Falls Convention advocated that women be granted "the rights and privileges
that belong to them as American citizens," just think about that,
equal pay for equal work. In 1872, Miss Victoria Woodhull, an
Ohioan, actually tried to run for President of the United States
with an African American Vice Presidential running mate, Freder-
ick Douglass. However, their Equal Rights Party name was removed from all state ballots before the national election.

In 1869, Cleveland's Forest City Club sponsored the city's
first professional baseball team. President Grant witnessing his
first baseball game was extremely impressed by "the most gentlemanly club in the country," when he viewed an exhibition performance by the Cleveland team. During the 1870 regular season, the
"gentlemanly" Forest City's were devastated by the New York
Athletics, 85 to 11.

Industrial expansion, innovation, opulence, poverty, and
corruption characterized America during the decades immediately following the Civil War. In a single generation the United
States moved from a second rate industrial nation into the world's
largest economic power.

To outfit Union military contingents, businesses enlarged
dramatically during the war. Fixed capital outlays (costs associated with the physical plant) overshadowed expenditures for
working capital (operating costs for labor, transport, and raw
materials). Because of the relative costs involved, these larger
companies were also more apt to continue operating during an
economic downturn, unlike their ante-bellum predecessors. With
the conflict resolved, these huge manufacturing enterprises retained the capacity to meet national demands rather than merely
supplying local markets.

As companies increased in size, they became more imper-
sonal, professional and more bureaucratic. Corporations expanded into new markets, operating in a multitude of cities.
Greater funds were allocated to research and development and
national advertising was used to encourage name recognition and
to promote consumer confidence.

Industrial consolidation continued throughout this era.
Two general strategies were employed to dominate specific
industries. Some companies sought to control all aspects of the

manufacturing process from the raw material to the finished product (vertical growth). Other businesses eliminated their rivals by controlling a product line (horizontal growth). Either strategy was designed to dissolve competition, leading to corporate control over a specific industry.

Ultimately, these monopolistic tendencies resulted in an unparalleled disparity of wealth. Luxurious estates became the norm in a few select areas, while the vast majority of Americans lived near the subsistence level. By 1909, the top one percent of the population had 47 percent of the total national wealth. Later the introduction of the income tax, federal legislation promoting competition, and the great depression resulted in a more equalized 20 percent controlling 46 percent of the national wealth by 1969. The inflationary 1970's and Reaganomics in the 1980's resulted in a concentration of wealth unparalleled since 1909. By 1989, the upper 1 percent of the population had 37 percent of the nation's wealth.

Waste, extravagance and greed often played a part in the manufacturing, shipping and pricing of goods necessary to supply the Union war effort. These discouraging and negative aspects of capitalism seemed to take precedence in post-bellum American business relationships. Unrestrained capitalism often utilized blackmail, bribery, intimidation, bogus companies, illegal rebates, pools and rate wars to foster an era of good stealing. Cleveland, the fastest growing city in America, witnessed the entire spectrum of these developments first hand.

John D. Rockefeller, amassed the world's greatest personal fortune by founding the Standard Oil Company in Cleveland during the 1870's. The Rockefeller family first moved into the area in 1853, briefly living in Strongsville and Parma before moving to Cleveland. John attended Cleveland Central High School, where he became friends with Mark Hanna and fell in love with his future wife, Laura Spelman.

At the age of nineteen, Rockefeller, a graduate of Folsom's Mercantile College (Dyke College), entered a wholesale commission partnership with Maurice B. Clark. In 1859, oil was discovered in Titusville, Pennsylvania and by the end of the Civil War, Cleveland had some thirty oil refineries. During the national conflict the partners began to invest their profits into oil refining. When an English candle-maker, Samuel Andrews, entered Cleveland with a new process to refine kerosene from crude petroleum, Rockefeller dissolved the partnership. While Clark retained control over a few refineries (Clark Oil), Rockefeller joined forces with Andrews and formed Standard Oil in 1870.

Executives of the firm and others began to build luxurious mansions along Cleveland's "Millionaire Row," Euclid Avenue. By the mid-1840's, 53 of the nation's 68 millionaires had homes on Euclid Avenue. Rockefeller's mansion was located at East 40th and Euclid Avenue while the former candle-maker built the largest home on the thoroughfare, "Andrews' Folly," which required over one hundred servants to maintain. Later Rockefeller built a summer home on his private estate, Forest Hills, in East Cleveland. Only a couple of magnificent estates remain on what was once described as "the most beautiful street in the world," by the world traveler and author, Baynard Taylor.

While touting high quality products, Standard Oil used pools, rebates, price wars, phony companies and its own barrels, barges and pipelines to gain control of some 75 refineries. Finally, threatening some two dozen competitors with a bankrupting price war, Rockefeller convinced his rivals to exchange their stock and control to Standard Oil, thus creating the nation's first trust. Ohio's opposition to these monopolistic tendencies forced Rockefeller to move his headquarters to New York. By 1890, Rockefeller controlled 90 percent of the production of oil in the country, becoming the world's first billionaire. The trust-busting Teddy Roosevelt forced the division of Standard Oil. Sohio, Standard Oil of Ohio, became an independent firm until it was purchased by British Petroleum in the 1980's. BP America's headquarters remain in the city, providing employment for over 2700 employees.

Cleveland's phenomenal growth after the Civil War was indebted to both expanded manufacturing opportunities and invention. Henry Sherwin, a dry goods clerk, teamed up with Edward Williams and A.T.Osborn to form Sherwin-Williams and Company in 1870. They refined the process of making paints and enamels by building grinders to pulverize pigments. Worcester Warner and Ambrose Swasey made machine tools of such precision that they earned world acclaim for their telescopes and turret lathes. Warner and Swasey telescopes developed such a reputation that they were used by the U.S. Naval Observatory and by an international clientele.

In 1879, Cleveland's Public Square became illuminated by the brightest lights known to man. On that April evening, Charles Brush demonstrated the superiority of his invention - the arc light. The following year he formed the Brush Electric Company to supply the city with street lighting. Behind his Euclid Avenue mansion, he built a windmill to operate over 400 batteries. Cleveland's weather is particularly well attuned to this type of power, since this area records more wind velocity than all other major metropolitan areas including Chicago (Dick Goddard). Undoubtedly, you may be questioning why Brush's commercial successor, the Illuminating Company, fails to use this inexpensive renewable energy source. The world's first electric streetcar began operating in Cleveland in 1884 utilizing the Brush dynamo. Ultimately, the Brush Electric Company and the Edison Illuminating Company merged to form the nucleus for the General Electric Company. In 1911, G.E. located her research center, the National Electric Lamp Association (NELA Park) in East Cleveland. NELA park is responsible for lighting most major national monuments including the Statue of Liberty and the Washington Monument.

In 1898, another Clevelander Alexander Winton built the first automobile ever sold in America. Responding to an ad in *Scientific American*, a mechanical engineer from Pennsylvania purchased the one-cylinder gasoline powered Winton for $1,000. Rollin White encouraged his father, Thomas White, the owner of White Sewing Machine Company, to invest in steam-and later petroleum-based vehicles, creating the White Motor Company. Walter Baker founded the Baker Motor Vehicle Company in 1898 to produce quieter electric cars. By 1900, six major auto-makers were producing vehicles in Cleveland.

Because of the pioneering efforts of Sherwin-Williams and Warner & Swasey, Cleveland continues to be a world leader in manufacturing of paints and machine tools. Ohio is the nation's largest manufacturer of trucks and second only to Michigan in the production of automobiles. Ford executives consider Cleveland as a "Second City" because of the size of their operations in Greater Cleveland. Major assembly facilities and parts suppliers like the Eaton Corporation, Standard Products and TRW, continue the legacy of Baker, Winton and White.

By the end of the century, Cleveland was the largest iron ore receiving port in the nation. In 1896, the first sighting of a serpentine Lake Erie monster was reported. At the turn of the century, the building of ore ships made the city the greatest ship building center in the United States.

During this era of mergers and consolidation, America was increasingly becoming a two-class society. America's fragmented and potentially antagonistic labor force was particularly vulnerable to corporate exploitation. Fledgling union organizations, threatened by strikebreakers, lockouts, yellow dog contracts, and corrupt and conservative courts, timidly concentrated their efforts upon uniting skilled labor.

General economic conditions and political repression

encouraged desperate Southern and Eastern Europeans to immigrate to the United States in unprecedented numbers. Unaware of the consequences of global interdependence, high US. tariff rates actually devastated much of Europe and unprotected American farmers. Low profit margins, two economic depressions during the 1870's and 1890's and monopolistic prices from manufactures and rail interests, simultaneously forced rural Americans to migrate in large numbers to major metropolitan areas.

Furthermore, the fear of losing employment heightened prejudices, particularly among native Americans and older immigrants toward the more recent urban inhabitants. This led to the creation of the anti-Catholic Know Nothing Party, later the Workingman's Party of California and in the 1880's the American Protective Association which became precursors to the anti-Catholic, anti-Semitic, anti-black, anti-oriental, and anti-immigrant Ku Klux Klan of the 1920's.

By contrast, Germany with a much more homogenous work-force provided illness and accident insurance, disability and retirement pensions for their workers by 1889. The United States did not adopt similar legislation until the Great Depression in 1935. Similarly, German workers, are protected from strike-breakers, have year-long parental leave, retraining programs for unemployed workers, a thirty-five hour workweek, and six weeks of paid vacation.

Philosophically, post-Civil War America accepted the "gospel of wealth." Capitalism provided the forum for a process of "natural selection." By applying the biological theories of Charles Darwin to man, Herbert Spencer's *Social Statistics* utilized scientific evidence to justify the elimination of a middle class. Monopolistic wealth was merely an example of the "survival of the fittest." Although Spencer's work never became a best seller, Horatio Alger's rags-to-riches stories popularized the potential for millions of Americans. These theories, which accepted the belief in the emergence of a superior social class, would ultimately be converted to justify repressive racial policies. The attempted genocide against the American Indians, the exclusion of Chinese immigrants, the introduction of Jim Crow laws in the South, and discriminatory immigration policies against Eastern Europeans by the National Origins Act can be traced to Spencer's conversion of Darwin's theory. American and European imperialism as well as both World Wars stem from these same thoughts.

Economic dominance led to selective corporate control over state and national policies. Often as a state's principal employer, company executives determined which law firms, financial institutions, newspapers, subcontractors, and business organizations would best suit the interests of the corporation. Endorsements, campaign donations and bribes enabled some businesses to unduly influence entire states. Anaconda Copper and the Southern Pacific Railroad were among the best or worst abusers in Montana and California respectively during this era. Contemporary examples of such dominance are rare. Only DuPont seems to have the same type of clout statewide.

Growing rural economic dissatisfaction led to creation of the Peoples Party. Advocating abandoning the gold standard, the direct election of US. Senators, the introduction of an income tax and the government regulation of heavy industry, the Peoples Party garnished over a million votes and 22 electors during the election of 1892. The success of the populists convinced conservative Southern entrepreneurs and politicians to advocate racial segregation to split white and black voters.

This led to the introduction of the Jim Crow laws in the South. Schools, recreational facilities, housing, cemeteries, hospitals, public transportation, and even doorways to public buildings were ordered segregated. In 1896, the US. Supreme Court upheld the constitutionality of the Jim Crow laws, in the case of *Plessy v. Ferguson*, naively believing the equal facilities would be provided for all. Two years later the Federal Court upheld the Southern conservatives introduction of a poll voting tax and literacy requirements in the case of *Williams v. Mississippi*. This established a general pattern of disenfranchising African Americans and defiant whites by introducing poll taxes and arbitrary literary tests.

Unlike their urban immigrant counterparts who found politics an avenue for employment, rural African Americans were encouraged to accept political non-participation. Booker T. Washington, the chief spokesman for African Americans, of whom 90 percent resided in the South, preached patience, conservatism and moderation. In the Atlanta Compromise of1895, Washington urged black Americans to accept the loss of political and social rights and strive for economic progress. As the head of an industrial training school in Alabama, the Tuskegee Institute, Washington felt that technical expertise alone would somehow overcome the barriers erected by white conservatives.

Urban African Americans were appalled at the introduction of the Jim Crow Laws and the implementation of voting restrictions in the South. Introducing the slogan "beauty is black," W.E.B. DuBois urged black Americans to preserve their cultural heritage by promoting their own literature, colleges and business. DuBois, the first black graduate from Harvard, founded the

Niagara Movement, 1905, and later the National Association for the Advancement of Colored People (NAACP) 1909, to promote political, social, and economic equality for African Americans. After nearly six decades of legal challenges, the NAACP successfully overturned the Plessy decision in *Brown v. the Board of Education of Topeka, Kansas*, 1954.

When the Democratic Party endorsed William Jennings Bryan and a similar populist platform in 1896, Marcus Alonzo Hanna, the Cleveland street car and steel magnate, marshaled corporate America to donate heavily to William McKinley, the Canton Republican nominee. Blanketing the nation with anti-Bryan propaganda and threatening job losses, the Republican candidate won. Similarly, in 1980, conservative interests donated through political action committees over $10,600,000, for Ronald Reagan's campaign, while raising less than $28,000, for President Carter's re-election and about $3,000, for John Anderson's third party effort.

Urban politics began to play an important role in gaining employment for the growing number of immigrants. Just as the moneyed interests managed to secure state or national dominance, ethnic voting blocs afforded a means to acquire recognition, political clout, and jobs. Machine politics and urban bossism emerged after the Civil War, paralleling the economic free-for-all which characterized this entire period.

Business concerns and bigotry convinced many former community leaders to pursue economic endeavors rather than actively participate in civic affairs. This exodus was quickly filled by self-indulgent politicians who utilized patronage, graft and municipal indebtedness to cater to the recently enfranchised immigrants. For some, public education provided the ladder for success. Others, finding restrictive hiring policies based upon prejudices, turned to bartering, exchanging services, petty or organized crime, or street peddling. However, machine politicians' emphasis upon rebuilding urban America provided employment based only on party loyalty. With the slow introduction of civil service, construction and public service jobs remained under the control of the boss.

By the end of the century, American cities were mired in corrupt machine politics. Patronage meant power, it made little difference which position the boss held. In New York, William Marcy Tweed was a member of the Board of Supervisors (county commissioner), in the District of Columbia, Alexander Shepherd headed the Board of Public Works and George B. Cox held no elective office when he controlled Cincinnati. Cleveland remained more typical with the reigns of power reserved to the mayor's office.

In 1895, a thirty-two year old Republican, Robert McKisson was elected mayor of Cleveland. Blinded by his own ambition to gain control of his party, he angered loyal business interests by attempting to build a political machine to oust Mark Hanna from the Republican hierarchy. Community leaders forged a reform minded Municipal Association to depose McKisson. Capitalizing upon these divisions within the Republican party "honest John" Farley, a former mayor and a Democrat, even received a campaign donation from Mark Hanna, in his successful campaign to unseat the "boy mayor" Robert McKisson. However, Farley's tenure was short-lived, alienating many residents when he requested the assistance of the state militia to maintain order during a streetcar strike in 1899 and his tacit acceptance of the loss of some $20 million of lakefront property to railroad interests ended his tenure after serving only one two-year term.

Table 1: Cleveland's Population 1800-1890

Year	Population
1800	7
1810	57
1820	606
1830	1,075
1840	6,071
1850	17,034
1860	43,417
1870	92,829
1880	160,146
1890	261,353

Source: Census Bureau

A GOLDEN AGE (1900-1929)

Once a year, as the pigeon droppings are removed from the statue of Tom Lofton Johnson, Clevelanders are reminded of a glorious past. Cleveland was brought to the pinnacle of fame and prominence by Tom L. Johnson. Under his tutelage, Cleveland inspired a national effort to eliminate machine politics as he championed a crusade against special interests and urban boss-ism. The city became the vortex for inspiring decency, honesty, efficiency, and good government in major metropolitan areas.

At the turn of the century, three mayors captured the imagination of urban America. Using a populist appeal, these mayors attacked municipal misfeasance and malfeasance in office by machine politicians; they introduced the progressive move-ment to urban politics. Hazen Pingree's Detroit became a model for eliminating graft and in Toledo, Samuel "Golden Rule" Jones, introduced merit examinations and the eight hour day to munici-pal employees, opened public playgrounds, kindergartens, and golf courses, liberalized parole policies, reformed the police department, gave temperance lectures to drunks, and created an open-air church available to all faiths. However, progressivism reached its zenith in Cleveland.

Tom L. Johnson originally entered Cleveland to take advantage of the multitude of street railways that operated within the city. Born in Kentucky, from a once-prosperous southern family, he became a newsboy at eleven, a millhand, and then a clerk for a transit line in Louisville at fifteen. That same year, Tom invented a farebox which netted him $30,000. While still in his teens, he purchased a mule driven railway in Indianapolis, and later he expanded his holdings into Buffalo and Cleveland. Soon he decided to concentrate his efforts on the most lucrative prize, the Forest City.

However, in Cleveland, his chief opponent for transit domination was the Republican champion, Mark Hanna. Both men competed bitterly to control the growing street car market. Their economic rivalries soon spilled over into basic philosophical and political beliefs. While Johnson envisioned public ownership of urban transit, Hanna remained committed to private owner-ship.

After reading Henry George's single tax theories in *Progress and Poverty*, Tom L. Johnson renounced his monopolistic ways and pursued a career in public service dedicated to end economic and social inequalities. Elected to Congress in 1887, he sought to reduce tariffs which artificially raised prices on manufactured goods. High tariffs benefited American industrialists but were detrimental to unprotected farmers and consumers. Johnson's activities reached national acclaim only when he became Cleveland's chief executive in 1901.

Deliberately arriving early on his first day, Johnson convinced the former mayor to relinquish the reigns of power to the newly elected city leader. This enabled Johnson to veto a bill which would have granted railroad interests $20 million worth of lake front property. Johnson's first official action was to reduce transit rates to three cents; although he fulfilled his campaign promise, legal challenges delayed enactment. Under Johnson, Cleveland became the first American city to have a municipally-owned street railway system. However, he failed to gain municipal ownership of all mass transit because the Chamber of Commerce, the Cleveland Electric Railway Company and other business interests successfully thwarted Johnson's transit initiatives.

Sadly, municipal control of the trolleys did not occur until 1942. By then, time and corporate profits had long before gutted the enterprise of its viability. Moreover, by the 1940's, General Motors was launching a diabolical attempt to destroy urban mass transit. GM sold petroleum-powered busses below there actual cost to unsuspecting cities. Without unsightly overhead wires or restrictive tracks, busses offered unimpeded travel throughout the metropolitan area. Once a city adopted the bus as the means of primary transport, the actual price appeared, services declined, and farebox prices rose dramatically. Many disenchanted commuters turned to an alternative form of transportation - the automobile. Although GM was found guilty in 1976, the Justice Department refused to punish the company that destroyed the type of non-polluting mass transit used by most developed countries. General Motors escaped punishment because it was determined that too much time had elapsed since the offense. This confrontation became the basis for at least one Academy Award winning film - "Who Framed Roger Rabbit."

After Johnson became mayor, Hanna entered politics. Elected to the Ohio General Assembly Hanna promoted legislation to dissolve urban governments throughout Ohio. Ultimately, the confrontations between Hanna and Johnson would exhaust both men. When Johnson announced his intention to run for governor; Hanna launched a grueling campaign that successfully defeated the Cleveland mayor in 1903. A grateful and obedient General Assembly elected Hanna to the United States Senate, but physically worn by the campaign ordeal, the Republican leader contracted typhoid fever and died shortly thereafter.

To meet the needs of Cleveland's expanding population, Johnson established a commission to plan a new West Side Market in 1901. Completed in 1912, the West Side Market catered to the city's divergent cultural and ethnic mosaic. During Johnson's eight years as mayor, he equalized taxation, built public tennis courts and playgrounds, reformed the penal code, introduced a comprehensive building code, annexed suburbs, and removed billboards. In addition, he successfully created a municipal electric power system; faced with city rates, which reduced costs by over a third, the Brush Electric Company lowered bills by 20 percent. It was Brush who developed the slogan "Cleveland, the best location in the nation."

Purchasing two thousand acres of inexpensive rural land for the aged, infirmed, and juvenile delinquents, Johnson inspired the growth of the "Emerald Necklace" which laid the foundation for one of the nation's premier natural recreational areas, the Cleveland Metroparks. Throughout the city, "Keep Off the Grass" signs were removed to encourage Clevelanders to take advantage of "their" greenery.

Lincoln Steffens was the principal critic of urban American politics during the turn of the century. In a series of articles for *McClures*, entitled "Shame of the Cities," he ridiculed and exposed municipal corruption throughout the nation. What Steffens found in Johnson's Cleveland was unique and he described the city as: "the best governed in the United States."

Cleveland's progressivism was not reserved to politicians. For many years the city's community and business leaders earned a national reputation for supporting a large number of philanthropic causes. In 1914, the Cleveland Foundation was established to combine these gifts to meet even larger needs. By consolidating small and large donations into a centrally administered organization, costs were reduced, frauds were eliminated, and more funds could be used for worthy health and welfare organizations. Supported by all faiths and nationalities, Cleveland's Community Chest became a national model, now known as the United Way. The city retains this noble tradition through her generosity, greater Cleveland's per capita donations to the United Way lead the nation for major urban areas.

Johnson was narrowly defeated in his attempt to win a fifth term as mayor in 1909, by Herman C. Baehr, the Republican challenger. Baehr, a German American, had earned a progressive reputation while serving as county recorder; however, after serving only one term, disappointed voters removed Baehr and revived the Johnson tradition by electing Newton D. Baker. Johnson, having committed nearly his entire fortune to municipally owned transit, was ousted from the mayor's office on the verge of success. His dream and personal wealth shattered, Johnson died in 1911, in a rented apartment.

Baker was Johnson's city solicitor, law director, and his closest advisor. As mayor, Baker persuaded Ohio's General Assembly to grant Cleveland home rule. Home rule permits an urban area the right to enact local ordinances, provide for municipal services, and determine what form of government the citizens desire. Setting up, electing, and implementing the recommendations of the Charter Commission took up much of Baker's tenure.

During the bitter debate over the election of the City Council, Cleveland's ethnic community successfully held out for a large council elected by individual wards. Baker's small council, voted at large, went down to defeat. Overall, Baker's success at winning home rule for the city won him national accolades and an appointment as Secretary of War under President Wilson in 1916.

In 1921, distrust toward ethnic ward politicians and growing evidence of corruption and graft led Cleveland residents to support a new charter, that adopted a City-Manager form of municipal government. Ostensibly, Cleveland became the largest city in the nation run by a City Manager when William R. Hopkins took over the helm of the city's government.

Normally, a City Manager is hired only after a thorough national search. This however did not happen in Cleveland. Instead, bosses divided patronage jobs between the two major parties. Although Hopkins a former councilman, improved roadways, enlarged parks, and brought Cleveland to the forefront of the aeronautical world by building the city's first airport, real power was retained by the party bosses.

Positively, Hopkins contributed to Cleveland's love affair with aviation. Although Charles Lindbergh's successful solo transatlantic flight in 1927 won him sudden fame, most Americans viewed the airplane as a novelty, something to be observed at barnstorming exhibitions during a county fair. Unlike much of America, Clevelanders became believers in the future of aviation. The National Air Races, NASA's Lewis Research Center, and the National Air Show at Burke Lakefront Airport all attest to the city's commitment to flight.

The inability of the city manager form of government to root out corruption convinced the city to return to mayoral control in 1931. After eight years of behind the scenes political maneuvering, the normally ineffective Democrats gained control of city hall, abolishing the city manager form of government.

The United States entry into World War One changed the fabric of urban America. Selective Service and massive wartime expenditures offered unprecedented job opportunities for women and rural African Americans. By the turn of the century, only four western states granted voting rights to women, however the pioneering efforts of Florence E. Allen and the "war to end war" finally convinced males to recognize Ohio's females as citizens.

After being denied admittance to Western Reserve University because of her sex, Allen earned a law degree at New York University and was admitted to the Ohio Bar in 1914. Serving as the Ohio Suffrage Party's attorney, Allen successfully defended East Cleveland's home rule charter, which granted voting privileges to women, before the Ohio Supreme Court in 1917. Allen became the nation's first female trial judge when she was elected to the Cuyahoga County Common Pleas Court in 1920. She became the first woman to serve on a State Supreme Court when elected to that position in 1922. Allen was named to the U.S. Court of Appeals by Franklin D. Roosevelt and later became the country's first female chief federal judge when she presided over the circuit court. The wartime accomplishments and the achievements of women like Florence Allen convinced the Ohio legislature to ratify the Nineteenth Amendment to the U.S. Constitution.

I believe voting is a cherished right, a privilege, and an obligation for all Americans. Anyone who misses two consecutive presidential election, without justification, is not living up to his or her civic responsibilities. Those who choose not to be a part of this nation's political life should be granted passage elsewhere. There are so many people worldwide who wish to be Americans, non-voters will be easily replaced, those who decide to remain should be considered aliens and made to reapply for citizenship.

During W.W.I. African Americans migrated from the rural South to the urban North. With immigration halted by the war, corporations desperate for manpower enticed blacks to leave the boll-weevil stricken South, with advertisements for lucrative job prospects. Urban streets were once again purported to be paved in gold.

Cleveland's African American population tripled between 1910 and 1920. For many, the promises were short-lived as returning veterans and a severe recession in 1921 quickly diminished employment opportunities. Progressivism had changed urban governments, unlike early immigrants who found employment through patronage, African Americans often found bosses and machine politics on the defensive and the introduction of merit examinations prevented any easy or automatic access to city service jobs. But the economic havoc wrought by the boll-weevil, and an overall decline in agricultural prices convinced most new arrivals to remain and encouraged more blacks to move into major metropolitan areas like Cleveland.

Table 2: Cleveland's African American Population
1910-1940

Year	Total Number	Percent
1910	8,448	1.5
1920	34,451	4.3
1930	71,899	8.0
1940	87,145	9.7

Source: Census Bureau

America entered the First World War for freedom, democracy, and humanity, but the Treaty of Versailles made a mockery of President Wilson's idea of peace without victory. Our European allies (associates) only wanted revenge after four years of unrelenting death and destruction, they were committed to punish the defeated. They ignored Wilson's ideas of self-determination, demanded punishing reparations from a vanquished Germany and expanded their colonial empires through the League of Nation's Mandates. A disillusioned U.S. Senate refused to ratify the Treaty of Versailles or become a party to the League of Nations. As a nation, our noble ideals were shattered; we felt betrayed.

Ultimately, our distrust toward Europe turned into a disdain for Europeans. Lenin's Bolshevik victory in Russia added a fear of Communism to this volatile mix. America wanted nothing more to do with Europe. In 1920, Republicans swept into power with slogans advocating isolationism and "America First".

Post-war immigrant protests and strikes were often viewed as anarchistic and communistic conspiracies. In 1919, the Federal Bureau of Investigation was founded by Wilson's Attorney General, A. Mitchell Palmer, to "drive from our midst the agents of Bolshevism." During the Red Scare, the FBI violated nearly every tenant of the U.S. Constitution that it was pledged to uphold as the Bureau's Palmer raids suspended the writ of habeas corpus and arrested without warrants some six thousand primarily Jewish, Russian Americans. Among those arrested, six-hundred were deported to the workers paradise-Russia.

By promoting ethnic, religious, and racial hatred, the Ku Klux Klan emerged as the enforcers of morality, prohibition, and fundamentalism. With cities outnumbering rural areas according to the 1920 census, nativists, fearing Armageddon, flocked to the Klan to defend "true American values." By 1923, the five largest Klans were located in Arkansas, Indiana, Ohio, Oklahoma, and Texas. Under the guise of "one-hundred percent Americanism," the Klan successfully fought to limit immigrants from Southern and Eastern Europe through the National Origins Act in 1924.

This distaste for things European took many forms. A large number of Americans came to believe that alcohol was the primary catalyst for W.W.I., because Germans brewed beer. Since America fought the Germans during the war, therefore eliminating alcohol, would prevent future wars. This kind of syllogistic logic helped to convince legislators to adopt the Eighteenth Amendment to the U.S. Constitution.

Opposition to prohibition in urban areas led to a growing disrespect towards the legal system and law enforcement fostering the growth of organized crime. Lucrative profits from untaxed, unregulated, and illegal liquor sales led to violence and gang wars for control of selective markets. As various ethnic groups vied for dominance within urban areas, anti-European hostility was reinvigorated since it appeared that Europe's wars were now being fought within the United States. The Saint Valentine's Day Massacre, the Black Sox Scandal, and introduction of speakeasies and jazz, merely confirmed what many Americans had already surmised: that America's cities were places of abhorrent violence, corruption and debauchery.

Cleveland has long been a part of organized crime. During the 1920's, conflicts over the control of corn sugar led to the Sugar Wars that left seventeen dead. In 1928, the first Mafia Grand Council meeting held at the Statler Hotel, was inadvertently broken up by an alert patrolman, Frank Osowski. Arrests, though quickly squashed by corrupt officials, succeeded in thwarting organized crime's first grand council from divvying up Cleveland's corn sugar monopoly. Three years later, open gang warfare would again erupt in the city.

Public indignation to the mounting violence nationwide convinced President Hoover to form the Wickersham Commission, 1929—1931, to study and make suggestions to improve the enforcement of criminal laws. Among the most important recommendations adopted from the work of the blue ribbon panel was the use of civil service exams rather than patronage as a basis of employment. The commission encouraged greater police specialization and emphasized appearance, courtesy, and efficiency. Crime and clearance rates were measured by the number of traffic tickets, juvenile offenders detained and arrested, illicit enterprises disrupted, and misdemeanor arrests made. These rates became the quantifiable variables of law enforcement. What was lost in this drive for efficiency was the role of a policeman as a peace officer. The film industry was forced to adhere to the Hollywood Code, which glorified the G-men (government agents) and enforced the notion that the bad guy never wins. It was not until the 1972 film "The Getaway" that Steve McQueen and Ally McGraw actually escaped with the loot.

No individuals did more to alter the face of Cleveland than the Van Sweringen brothers. Oris Paxton and Mantis James Van Sweringen began their career by opening a bicycle shop. Soon they became involved in land speculation in Lakewood but bankruptcy convinced them that profitable real estate endeavors had to be linked to a street car line. After success in Cleveland Heights, the Van Sweringens designed Shaker Heights as the "largest and wealthiest real estate subdivision in the United States." The strict enforcement of building codes limited commercial activities to one acre, mandated a minimum cost of $17,500, and provided that no two homes could be built alike along the broad park-like residential avenues, which made Shaker Heights the most exclusive suburb in America, until surpassed by Gross Point, Michigan, in 1960.

Table 3: Early Suburban Growth in Cleveland 1910-1940

Year	Cuyahoga County	% within Cleveland
1910	637,425	88
1920	943,495	74
1930	1,201,455	75
1940	1,217,250	72

Source: Census Bureau

Most transit lines began at Public Square and terminated in a circular fashion at an upscale housing location, like the Ridgewood development around the Parma Circle. Occasionally, some trolleys ended at an amusement park like Puritas Springs or Euclid Beach. The golden age of the wooden roller coasters was made to order for the daredevil 20's, while the big band era kept dance halls located at the parks swinging through the 30's and 40's. More distant amusement areas like Geauga Lake and Cedar Point often relied upon automobile, bus, train or excursion boat travel for vacationing patrons. The trolley line was the essential link to economic success as the saga of the Van Sweringens aptly demonstrated.

Their inability to be granted a right-of-way for a rapid transit line from the eastern suburb to Public Square led Van Sweringens on one of the most amazing adventures in the annals of American business. They purchased the Nickel Plate Railroad from the New York Central Railroad to give them access to downtown Cleveland. When the Pennsylvania Railroad refused to move their depot to meet the Shaker Rapid, the Van Sweringens decided to build their own union station. They built the largest and tallest building outside of New York City, the Terminal Tower, the fifty-two story "wonder of the mid-west" remained the tallest building outside of New York until 1967.

To maintain the profitability of the Terminal Tower and the Nickel Plate, the brothers constructed a department store, Higbee's (Dillard's) and a hotel, the Cleveland Hotel (Stouffer's Tower City Plaza Hotel) flanking the edifice, and set the footers for a third wing behind the union station. Simultaneously, they began a bewildering spending spree, financed by exuberant bankers and a complicated maze of pyramidal holding companies, O.P. and M.J. acquired 24 railroads and a total of 231 companies with a book value of four billion dollars before the stock market crash. Although they surveyed their railroad empire in one of three luxurious Pullman cars and lived in a 660 acre estate in Hunting Valley, Daisy Hill, the Van Sweringens actual net worth was only about $500,000.

Much of Cleveland's economic diversity was indebted to Cyrus Stephen Eaton. Cyrus arrived in Cleveland from Nova Scotia, at the age of nineteen with 20 dollars in his pocket. He came to the city to spend the summer with his uncle, the minister of the Euclid Avenue Baptist Church, the Reverend Charles Aubury Eaton. The young man worked in a variety of capacities for the most prominent member of his uncle's congregation, John D. Rockefeller who also served as a Bible school teacher at the church. Turning down a full-time job at Standard Oil, Cyrus returned to Canada to complete his divinity studies at McMaster University. After spending the following summer as a cowboy in

Saskatchewan, Eaton returned to minister to the Lakewood Baptist Church.

When Rockefeller asked Cyrus to return to his relatively under developed homeland to obtain utility franchises, he complied. Soon thereafter, the oil magnet withdrew his support for a electric plant in Brandon, Canada but Eaton successfully continued the project. Once the project was operational, he sold his holdings for a profit. One franchise led to another and by 1914, Eaton was a millionaire two-fold. In 1930, Eaton sold his combined gas and electric holdings to Samual Insull's Chicago Commonwealth Edison Company for 56 million dollars. Shortly after the stock market debacle, Insull's utility empire collapsed.

Eaton merged a half dozen steel companies into the third largest steel producer in the United States, Republic Steel (LTV). While attempting to consolidate his holdings with Bethlehem Steel, Eaton and many Cleveland investors lost millions after the 1929 crash, which led many community leaders to blame Cyrus for their financial plight. Generally, Eaton was viewed as an outsider by many of Cleveland's business elite.

In addition to his steel and utility enterprises, he had working control of Goodyear Tire and Rubber, and sizable holdings in Firestone and Goodrich. Eaton was in the process of merging the three companies when the market crashed. In 1929, Cyrus was worth over $100,000,000. When the financial calamity ended, Eaton's net worth was reduced to $100,000.

THE ABYSS (1929-1945)

As the Terminal Tower reached toward the clouds and the Cleveland Stadium emerged from her subterranean hideaway, someone noticed a slight haze and a brief reflection. It was as if Penn and Teller had unmasked another secret of prestidigitation. The magic was gone, what remained exposed and uncovered was the smoke and mirrors of the narcissistic 1920's.

Although the failed financial dealings of the Van Sweringens and Cyrus Eaton took an astonishing fiscal toll on Cleveland's banking and social elite, their activities were merely symptomatic of the speculative nature of much of the economic growth of the 20's. By utilizing a technique known as buying on margin, many Americans began to invest in the stock market surge of the 1920's. With as little as a 5 percent down, often with homes, automobiles and furniture serving as collateral and stock certificates held in escrow provided the remaining equity, inflated investment opportunities boosted the stock market to resounding heights.

Buying on margin artificially increased stock prices but did not increase employment. As too many dollars chased too few stock offerings, capital ventures and new job opportunities declined. As long as new investors could be found, stock prices and paper profits increased. However, buying on margin had a potentially catastrophic downside. A request for payment, a margin call, after a market downturn of, say, 7 percent could have resulted in the loss of all tangible assets. Despite the risks, thousands of small investors became caught up in the "Great Bull Market" of the 20's.

In October, 1929, prices on the New York Stock Exchange plummeted. Panicked investors dumped their holdings. Billions were lost in the selling frenzy that followed. Yet the stock market crash did not cause the Great Depression. Something was fundamentally wrong with the American economy. Just as the Twenties set the stage for the Great Depression of the Thirties, the Eighties sowed the seeds for the economic reversals of the Nineties. A comparison between the Twenties and Eighties is frightening. During the Eighties, we managed to duplicate the defects in the economy that caused the Great Depression.

Consolidation of industry increased in the 1920's. The elimination of competition often creates short term profits through layoffs and unemployment, but pursued as a general course of action this correspondingly reduces the possibility of a quick recovery. Junk bonds in the 1980's pursued these same objectives all in the name of quarterly returns.

During the Twenties, some basic American industries, i.e. coal, textile and shoe, entered a period of decline. In the Eighties, foreign competition continued to threaten even more basic components of our consumer economy. Agriculture represented a fundamental weakness in the American economy in the 20's as high debt and low profit margins threatened American farmers' livelihood. Many family farms were essentially collectivized under the control of agribusiness in much of the Midwest due to the same fundamental problems during the 1980's.

During the latter half of the Twenties, as in the Eighties, the automobile industry leveled-off and there was also an overall decline in construction and in the number of workers in labor unions. Anti-union sentiment weakened organized labors position in collective bargaining, which could have helped abrogate the growing disparity of wealth, during both eras. Similarly, there were no new major boom industries introduced to stimulate consumer interest. Corporate salaries and profits remained exorbitantly high. As advertising and easy credit encouraged increasing individual purchases and debt, wealth became concentrated into too few hands. Productivity expanded rapidly during both decades, advancing 50 percent during the 20's, as automation and employee cutbacks increased profit margins.

Andrew Mellon, the Secretary of the Treasury, during the Twenties, reduced taxes for the wealthiest Americans, while raising tariffs on consumer goods. A million dollar tax burden was reduced from $660,000 in 1920, to $200,000, in 1927. This gave every millionaire nearly a half million dollars a year to automate, to advertise, to speculate on real estate or the stock market, or to indulge in luxury consumption. Individuals were encouraged to do everything to make money, except to provide employment. During the Eighties income taxes were reduced from $500,000 in 1980, to $280,000 in 1987 for each million. This gave every millionaire a 44 percent tax reduction, a windfall to similarly indulge in non-productive endeavors. At the same time, Social Security, state, and local taxes were increased, to eliminate similar reductions to middle income American families.

Paralleling the 20's, the 80's witnessed a massive increase in speculative investments in foreign loans, the stock market and real estate. With government encouragement, major lending institutions granted loans to Third World countries, loans that became increasingly uncollectable with the widening global economic downturn. Though small investors were not the principal losers in the bull market collapse in 1987, unlike 1929, all Americans became the victims. Major stock market manipulators made fortunes during both market upswings. In the late 1980's Michael Milken and Ivan Boesky sold junk bonds to Savings and Loans that had overextended themselves in the building boom of the 1980's. The S&L bailout increased the U.S. deficit for each and every taxpayer by five thousand dollars. Overall, these policies weakened our remaining financial institutions to the point that banks refused most corporate loans, while lower interest rates have encouraged banks to purchase government bonds or their former banking competitors. Vacant buildings and office space remain in our cities and suburbs, standing as a monument to the extravagances of the 1980's in the 1990's.

Finally, today's Federal Reserve Board seems unable to foster growth, as did its counterpart in the 30's. Although, the present Board behaved far more responsibly during the boom years than its predecessor, it still has not realized that the shrinking investment base within the U.S. banking industry is greatly due to bank mergers and to depositors withdrawing savings and investing in higher yielding U.S. savings bonds, the stock market and mutual funds and refinancing home mortgages.

Psychologically, the stock market crash became the catalyst for the Great Depression. The crash symbolized a loss of confidence in the basic economic future of the United States. Businesses and consumers sought to insulate themselves from the economic calamity, employers laid off workers to reduce labor costs and consumers cut back purchases. Fearful employees, the under employed and the unemployed curtailed spending to the bare essentials. As business and consumer confidence ebbed, more cuts followed, resulting in even less employment, more uncertainty, and even more consumer restraint. A perpetual downward spiral ensued, remarkably similar to the late Eighties and early Nineties.

An isolationist America seemed totally oblivious to the fact that a depression had already spread across Europe. World War One had burdened the victors with gigantic debts and punished the vanquished with unrealistic war reparations, and social and economic dislocation. The Treaty of Versailles arbitrarily blamed Germany for the conflict. Therefore, Germany was ordered stripped of her former colonial empire, divided by the Polish Corridor to Danzig, and expected to pay $50 billion (with interest) in redress to the victors. Interest on German reparation payments to France and Belgium increased to more than the two counties were worth in 1914. In an effort to meet the unreasonable demands of the allies, Germany's fledgling democratic government, the Weimar Republic, dramatically inflated the currency. This oft-used ploy seldom works in international debt repayment. In 1923, Belgium and French forces seized the German Rhineland and Ruhr basin for non-payment of reparations.

During the economic chaos that followed the devaluation of the Deuschemark, the United States, feeling somewhat at fault, loaned the Weimar Republic $2.6 billion under the Dawes Act. Germany's surrender in W.W.I was based upon the belief in Woodrow Wilson's Fourteen Points, which sought to guarantee an impartial settlement of colonial claims, self determination, and peace without victory. However, the Dawes Act loans were diverted from the Weimar Republic to the allies in reparations. Since the allies used the German payments to repay war debts and purchase American goods, the United States, in actuality began financing her own export trade. The dominant position of the United States economy in the world escaped no one except the U.S. herself.

Newly formed representative governments in Eastern Europe fared no better as ethnic rivalries, class conflicts and economic dislocation characterized most of this area after the "Great War." Carved out of the former Russian and Austro-Hungarian Empires, these embryonic republics rapidly degenerated into an amalgamation of economic basket cases and authoritarianism.

Unaware of the global nature of the depression, President Herbert Hoover and Congress attempted to raise government revenues by increasing tariff rates through the Hawley-Smoot Tariff of 1930 and by canceling the Dawes Act. The prohibitive nature of the Hawley-Smoot Tariff effectively canceled America's import trade, and actually reduced tariff revenues. These trade restrictions unintentionally encouraged Japanese militarists to invade China and seize Manchuria in 1931. The termination of the Dawes Act annihilated what remained of the German economy. Due to the fiscal collapse, the Weimar Republic stopped paying reparations, which in turn halted European debt repayment and purchases of American exports. During the political paralysis which followed, Adolph Hitler became Chancellor of the Weimar Republic in 1933. By 1935, Hitler was in total command in Germany and the Nazi era had begun.

As Fascism and authoritarianism spread across Europe and Asia, The United States retreated further into isolationism. During the mid-Thirties, many Americans came to believe that we had been tricked in World War One by the massive purchase of war material by the allies from US companies who served as the merchants of death. Clevelander's Joe Shuster and Jerry Siegal, developed the concept of the premier American superhero, *Superman*. Syndicated in hundreds of newspapers and several comic books, *Superman's* earliest villains included war profiteering merchants of death when he first appeared in the late 1930's.

In response to Fascist Italy's invasion of Ethiopia, the United States passed the Neutrality Act of 1935, which forbade arms sales to billigerents. Benito Mussolini's well armed forces were able to defeat the poorly equipped Abyssinian defenders. When the Fascist forces of General Francisco Franco, backed by Hitler and Mussolini, launched an attack against the democratically elected Spanish Republic, Congress broadened the Neutrality Act to encompass civil wars. Germany and Italy, officially noncombatants, could purchase U.S. goods on a "cash and carry" basis. Once again, U.S. policy contributed to the spread of fascism, since the Republics only supporter, the Soviet Union, was unable to purchase American goods because of unresolved tsarist debts.

President Franklin Roosevelt was finally able to avoid the restrictions imposed by the Neutrality Act when Japan invaded China from Manchuria in 1937. Since neither side declared war, the United States overwhelmingly supported China, while allowing only token sales to the Japanese aggressors. Although Americans supported the President's actions in Asia, they remained preoccupied with our domestic economic dilemma and generally unconcerned with world events and foreign policy issues.

The United States was totally unprepared for the economic abyss into which this nation would plummet during the depression. Densely populated major cities, with large concentrations of vulnerable commercial and industrial concerns, were particularly hard hit by the Great Depression. Cleveland, the sixth largest city in the nation, faced a record number of business and financial failures and unparalleled unemployment during the 1930's.

However, the city's diversified manufacturing base offered at least some employment. Further a few massive building projects started during the 20's like the Terminal Tower complex and the Cleveland Stadium provided employment for some Clevelanders. Over 80,000 Clevelanders witnessed the first game played by the Cleveland Indians in their new stadium in 1932. From 1891 to 1932, the Indians played at League Park. The Cleveland Indians derive their name from Louis Francis Sockalexis, a Penobscot Indian who played for the Cleveland Spiders from 1897-1899. In 1914, a newspaper contest adopted the name from a fan who wanted to honor "Chief" Sockalexis. Other smaller building projects also contributed to short term employment as well as to decades of future enjoyment. A permanent home for the Cleveland Orchestra, Severance Hall, was donated to the city through the generosity of John Severance, in 1930 and the Cleveland Arena, home to the Cleveland Barons and numerous sporting events, was constructed in 1937.

The depression also began to cut into bootlegging profits. With revenues in decline, consolidation and control became the order of the day in many American cities. In Cleveland Neapolitan and Sicilian factions fought a vicious gang war known as the Castellamarese War. Frank Milano, the leader of the Mayfield Road Mob, was given a seat on the Mafia's seven-member national commission in 1931. The factional conflict ended when both sides agreed to accept the commission's judgment in 1932. Milano's reign was short lived, however, as Cleveland's organized crime leader fled to Mexico in 1934 to avoid federal tax agents. During the federal crackdown, two rum-running lake captains, Philip and Charles Stakes, a father and son duo, were also forced to relinquish their vessels to avoid incarceration. Alfred "Big Al" Polizzi succeeded Milano as the head of the Mayfield Road Mob. As a veteran of the prohibition, Sugar and Castellamarese wars, Polizzi reigned as the head of organized crime in Cleveland for ten years.

The ratification of the 21st Amendment to the U.S. Constitution which repealed prohibition dramatically reduced the illicit profits of La Cosa Nostra (in 1932, the commission adopted La Cosa Nostra, "our thing" as the official title for the Mafia). Further, the public outcry against organized crime after the Castellamarese blood bath resulted in the election of Harold Burton, a reform mayor. Burton forced the syndicate out of Cleveland by outlawing gambling within the city limits and he appointed a new Safety Director, Eliot Ness, whose indictments forced many Mafia figures to flee Cleveland.

Big Al moved the mob's slot machines and casino operations to neighboring communities, among them the Harvard Club in Newburgh Heights, the Thomas Club in Maple Heights, the Mounds Club in Lake County and the Pettibone and Arrow Clubs in Geauga County. Polizzi was the first crime leader to invest in legitimate businesses as prohibition and gambling revenues were invested in Las Vegas hotels and casinos, and in Polizzi Construction in Florida. In addition, Big Al introduced the nation's first wire service to allow gambling on sports events. In 1944, Polizzi retired and moved to Miami. Years later, highly questionable workmanship by his construction company inspired a made for TV mini-series, "Condominium."

In an ordinary transition of power, John Scalish assumed the mantel of mob leadership. Tough, respected and pragmatic, Scalish ruled Cleveland's underworld for over three decades uniting the major Jewish and Italian crime factions principally through wedding vows. The financial wizard of Cleveland's Mafia, Maishe "Milton" Rockman, married Scalish's sister. In turn, Scalish married Rockman's sister, and Angelo Lonardo, the under-boss of the mob, also married a sister of Scalish. However, this close-knit family arrangement left little opportunity for advancement for the powerful lieutenants of Cleveland's Mafia.

Cleveland's crime community increasingly suffered from attrition and public exposure, ambitious younger members of the mob left the city for greener pastures. After the Senate Organized Crime (Kefauver) Committee hearings in 1950 and the federal raid of a national meeting of crime lords, held in Appalachia, New York in 1957, many of the nations and the city's top leaders were "uncovered." Real opportunities would have to wait until Scalish was out of the picture.

Eliot Ness recorded only one noteworthy failure while serving as Safety Director: his inability to prosecute the "butcher of Kingsbury Run." Between 1935 and 1938, a dozen individuals, mostly transients, were literally butchered by an unknown assailant. During the 30's, without any county, state, or national networking to exchange information, local police forces worked in solitude. Therefore, when the murderer's first victims, two Parma schoolteachers, Louise Wolf and Mabel Foote, were found brutally slashed to death in 1921, no countrywide effort was made to correlate these deaths to the torso slayings a dozen years later.

After the Parma murders, six mutilated victims, some decapitated, were uncovered near New Castle, Pennsylvania, between 1925-1934. The Cleveland murders began in 1935, and lasted until 1938. During this period portions of a dozen dismembered corpses were discovered. Now known as the torso murders, most of the victims were last seen alive near the railroad yard at Kingsbury Run. Ness' solution, greatly criticized at the time, was to destroy the dwelling used by the homeless near the railroad tracks where most of the victims were last known to reside. The killings stopped in Cleveland but the perpetrator was never apprehended.

However, six more decapitated and dismembered bodies were uncovered along the railroad lines that led back toward Pennsylvania, between 1939 —1942. Elizabeth Short, nicknamed the Black Dahlia, was the first of seven similarly mutilated individuals discovered around Los Angeles in 1947. Could a single serial killer have murdered all 33 over a 26 year period? Fifty years later, all of these homicides still remain unsolved.

Eliot Ness succeeded in bringing about the first major reformation of the Cleveland Police Department. Under Ness, the city was divided into five police districts and foot patrols were replaced by radio-dispatched vehicles to promote efficiency. However, he failed to root out corruption within the department. Years later, the Safety Director found out why. One of Ness' top aides, a police lieutenant, had been on the mob's payroll leaking information to the syndicate.

Burton remained mayor until 1940, when he was elected to the United States Senate. Cleveland would not elect another Republican mayor for thirty years. Burton would later be appointed to serve on the U.S. Supreme Court. His Safety Director, already famous for his tireless efforts against Al Capone in Chicago, continued to receive national accolades for his determination to drive organized crime out of Cleveland.

Despite the depression, Cleveland became the focal point for national politics. The successes of Harold Burton and Eliot Ness brightened the city's public image. More importantly, Jesse Owens, an African American Clevelander, captured four gold metals during the 1936 Berlin Olympics. Owens earned the title of "the world's greatest living athlete" as he repeatedly defeated Hitler's "master race," breaking three world records in the process. In 1936, both the Republican and the Union Party held their national conventions at Cleveland's Public Auditorium. In June, the Great Lakes Exposition opened to the public. Over four million visitors attended the opening year of the extravaganza, including President Roosevelt. Expanded in 1937, the Exposition poured $30 million into the city. In addition, the National Air Races attracted thousands to Cleveland's lake front during the Labor Day holidays.

In 1939, 1941, and 1945, the Cleveland Barons won the American Hockey League Championship. Also in 1945, the city's black baseball team, the Cleveland Buckeyes won the World Series in the African American League.

As baseball began to integrate after the Second World War, premier players like Cleveland's Sam Jethroe were recruited by teams like the Boston Braves. During his first season with the Braves, Jethroe became the National League's Rookie of the Year. The Cleveland Indians became the first American League (AL) team to intergrate, when owner Bill Veeck signed the first black player in the AL, Larry Doby, on July 3, 1947. The final game for the Buckeyes was played in 1950.

President Roosevelt's "New Deal" provided employment opportunities for some Clevelanders. Between 1935 and 1939, the Works Progress Administration (WPA) funded nearly $5 million into improvements to the Cleveland Public Schools. Numerous improvements were also made by the WPA to enhance the Metropolitan Park System, including expanding the Cultural Gardens, developing Forest Hill Park (the land having been donated by John D. Rockefeller Jr.) and building pavilions, access routes, and bridges throughout the Metroparks. And the Public Works Administration provided funding for new housing projects and supplemented expenditures for the Main Avenue Bridge across the Cuyahoga River.

Ultimately, Americas forced entry into World War Two mandated the massive expenditures necessary to end the depression in order to defend the country. Faced with a tangible enemy, the United States finally accepted the concepts of the British economist, John Maynard Keynes. Keynes suggested that a country should spend its way out of a depression by using deficit spending. Once confidence and government revenues returned to normal, Keynesian economics called for tax increases to eliminate the national debt. Japan's surprise attack at Pearl Harbor not only convinced the United States to become an active participant in the alliance against fascism and totalitarianism, but it also provided the impetus for the government to spend the money necessary to end the Great Depression.

War production and the draft once again opened employment opportunities. As business and labor concentrated on military needs, consumer goods were placed on the back burner. Once the conflict was resolved, pent-up demand kept the post-war American economy generally on course. Corporate profits, union membership, marriages and the city's birth rate were all on the upswing as a patriotic Cleveland looked optimistically toward the end of the war.

The Second World War devastated Europe, China and Japan. Emerging from the carnage were two new mutually suspicious and potentially hostile military powers, the United Sates and the Soviet Union, and their differing ideologies and interests would soon evolve into the Cold War. But for America and Cleveland, the war was over, and the future configuration of the world was not our concern.

KEEPING UP WITH THE JONES' (1945-1962)

Returning veterans collectively seemed to have missed some thing during their years of military service. Perhaps it may have been radio shows like "Jack Benny," "Gang Busters," or "The Shadow," or maybe small screen television sets - well for whatever reason, Cuyahoga County's population increased by over 26 percent between 1939 and 1959. The baby boom transformed urban America after the Second World War, at first ballooning the population of central cities and then it burst into the suburbs.

Early attempts by the Federal government to provide temporary housing projects could not keep up with the surge in demand. Most of these projects were scattered to the city's outer rim but prospective home buyers soon overwhelmed the market place. Forced savings necessitated by the wartime deficiency of consumer goods enabled many American families the wherewithal to purchase their own homes. Additionally, military severance checks and Federally guaranteed low interest loans made available by the Federal Housing Administration (FHA), the G.I. bill and the Veterans Administration (VA) encouraged a sellers market in real estate. When Federal price controls were lifted, only one ingredient was missing to complete the mix: an adequate means of transportation.

World War Two revolutionized transportation within the United States. Prior to the War, urban transit was served almost exclusively by trolleys. Though an ever-increasing number of individuals possessed automobiles, parking, congestion and inadequate roadways prevented their utilization. Travel between cities remained dominated by railroads. Asian and European journeys were often reserved for the wealthy who could afford an extended holiday on an ocean liner.

The building of an interstate highway system funded by the Federal Highway Act of 1956, dramatically altered urban society. In Cleveland alone, entire neighborhoods were eradicated as thousands of homes were destroyed to build the interstate system. Over the next two decades, I-90 (1959—1978), I-71 (1963—1968), and I-77 (1959—1973), devastated much of the Irish, Italian and Polish communities within the city, as over fifteen percent of the total housing units in Cleveland were eliminated between 1959 and 1979.

Technological advancements made during the war in

aviation swiftly became available for civilian application. These developments, which added to the safety, range, and size of aircraft, fundamentally altered the nation's long distance travel, ultimately relegating ocean liners and railroads to a second or third class status. Larger airplanes and increased demand forced airports to extend their runways and capacity. Jet propulsion, another by-product of the war, soon added another element, noise. This combination of factors prompted the removal of even more nearby dwellings.

Additionally, the Housing Act of 1949, encouraged Federally funded urban renewal projects. Unlike the New Deal's housing programs which restricted funding to public housing, this act left development decisions to local authorities. The Forest City launched the nation's largest urban renewal effort during the 1950's. Anticipating a rapid influx of private investment dollars, Cleveland leveled over 6,000 acres of east side inner-city neighborhoods. Although some subsidized public housing units were constructed, local development funds for middle class housing failed to materialize. Thousands of inner city residents, mostly black, were forced to migrate into the only housing available as blockbusters took advantage of the tremendous opportunities to subdivide and rent larger homes in areas like Glenville and Hough. Inflamed by rumors, panicked home owners often sold their properties for a fraction of its actual value. "White flight" was a phenomenon caused by cement and perception rather than a noticeable increase in African American immigration into the city.

Table 4: Housing Units in Cleveland 1950-1990	Year	Total Number	Percent of change
	1950	270,943	7.8%
	1960	282,914	4.3%
	1970	264,100	-6.7%
	1980	239,587	-9.3%
	1990	224,311	-6.4%

Source: Census Bureau

The post-war era also witnessed a fundamental change in production techniques. Prior to the war it was not uncommon for manufacturing plants to utilize a single multi-floored vertical structure to produce a product. After the war a growing number of American companies began to use the moveable assembly line in a more horizontal fashion which required large tracks of afford-

43

able land. Taking advantage of the relatively inexpensive land available in the suburbs, these new plants were increasingly constructed outside of the central city.

Developers were no longer restrained by the steel rail and the overhead electric lines of the trolley system and quickly took advantage of the interstate highway system. Soon thereafter, the automobile became a necessity of suburban life. Job opportunities spurred on by airport and corporate expansion into the suburbs encouraged an outward migration away from urban core.

Gradually retail establishment began to follow the urban exodus. A few small shopping areas emerged in the suburbs often anchored by food stores like A&P or Fisher Foods. Following the leadership of Sears, Roebuck and Company and Federal's, downtown department stores ventured into the suburbs. Locally the retailers who joined the outward migration Halle Brother's, the Higbee Company (Dillard's) and the May Company (Kaufmann's) survived, at least until the acquisition oriented 80's and 90's Those who remained in their cozy downtown hideaway, Bailey's, Sterling-Linder and Taylor's, were doomed. Recently the building of upscale retail outlets like the Galleria and the Avenue at Tower City have provided a resurgence in downtown shopping (Tower City was actually constructed upon the footers left by the Van Sweringens who envisioned a third wing for the Terminal Tower Complex).

Surging populations enabled many suburbs to take advantage of the state's home rule provisions. Cleveland's early expansion was often gained through suburban annexation. Home rule restricted this growth; soon the Forest City was surrounded by suburban enclaves. Geographically, Cleveland extends only 79 square miles. By comparison, Columbus, the state's largest city, contains 190 square miles but only 961,437 live in the state capital's Franklin County, while 1,412,140 reside in Cleveland's Cuyahoga County.

Politically, Franklin County votes Republican, whereas Cuyahoga County votes Democratic. Because of Cleveland's diminutive land area, suburbs that border on the city and those along the earliest completed interstate I-71, tend to vote Democratic while those beyond the inner ring and the I-71 corridor tend to vote Republican. Between 1952 and 1988, suburbs have generally voted Republican in national elections. In 1992, President Clinton won a plurality of the suburban vote. If this victory represents a new trend in voting, it could significantly alter national voting patterns, since more Americans live in suburbs than in central cities according to the 1990 census. It should be noted, that the third party candidacy of Ross Perot captured 20 percent of the suburban vote in 1992.

Table 5: Suburban Growth - Cuyahoga County 1950-1990		
Year	Cuyahoga County	% within Cleveland
1950 ——	1,389,532 ——	65.8
1960 ——	1,647,895 ——	53.1
1970 ——	1,720,835 ——	43.6
1980 ——	1,498,400 ——	38.3
1990 ——	1,412,140 ——	35.8

Source: Census Bureau

The post war-era also witnessed the reemergence of Cyrus Eaton. Eaton survived the depression by retaining control of a small investment firm, Otis and Company. During the 1940's he risked everything he owned on an incredible gamble when he attempted to drain a four mile wide fifteen mile long lake and retrieve the iron ore deposits supposedly located below. Under Steep Rock Lake, Eaton found the principal sources of high grade iron ore in North America. By 1958, his Ungava Iron Ore Company had ten billion tons of reserves leading *Fortune* to proclaim Cyrus Eaton, "the iron master of North America."

A friend of organized labor, Cyrus borrowed money from the United Mine Workers to purchase the Western Kentucky and Nashville Coal Companies. What industrialist could obtain a loan from a labor union today? During the 1960's he purchased the Cincinnati and Ohio Railroad and merged it with the Baltimore and Ohio Railroad forming the most profitable railroad in the United States - the Chessie System. Coal from his mines traveled his rails to the Cleveland Electric Illuminating Company (CEI). Eaton was also a major stockholder in CEI. Using his over two and a half billion dollar collection of railroads, iron and coal mines, steel mills, manufacturing enterprises, construction and real estate holdings and utilities, he was able to boost Cleveland Trust into a dominant banking position in Ohio.

Although many decision shapers continued to hold a deep-seated resentment toward Eaton because of the stock market debacle, Eaton remained active in community affairs. Eaton was a major contributor to Metropolitan Park Board (Metroparks), the Cleveland Health Museum, and the Cleveland Museum of Natural History. As a strong supporter of the YMCA evening school, Eaton assisted in the creation of Fenn College and later Cyrus helped in the transformation of Fenn College into Cleveland State University.

Eaton's political views also antagonized many within Cleveland's conservative business community. Nikita Khrushchev's decision to unilaterally withdraw Soviet forces in Austria set in motion what would become known as the "Spirit of Geneva." During the first post-war summit, the Cold War leaders agreed to encourage future agricultural, cultural, scientific and technological exchanges. During one of these exchanges a group of Soviet agricultural experts were sent to the United States and Cyrus was asked by the Eisenhower administration to entertain the Russian delegates at his Northfield estate Acadia Farms, which was nationally known for breeding prize-winning Black Angus cattle.

This meeting transformed Eaton into a laborer for world peace. For his commitment to global understanding and nuclear disarmament, he was awarded the Lenin Peace Prize in 1960. His companies designed and constructed a number of western style hotels in the Soviet Union and in Cuba, the latter through Canadian subsidiaries. Always a capitalist, Eaton demanded payment up front for these projects. After President Nixon's triumphant journey to the People's Republic of China, the Nixon administration tried to use Eaton's good offices to open a similar dialogue with Fidel Castro but this effort failed when a group of Cubans fled into Guantanamo Bay. Most local business leaders remained baffled by Eaton's endeavors.

A winning major league team often makes citizens feel good about their city, therefore a successful sports season often benefits an incumbent mayor. Clevelanders had a lot to feel proud about during the immediate postwar period. From 1945 to 1950, the city's teams provided residents with an assortment of national championships. The victorious seasons for the Barons and the Buckeyes in 1945, were followed by major league victories for both the Cleveland Indians and the Cleveland Browns. In 1948, the Cleveland Indians captured the American League Pennant and defeated the Boston Red Sox to win the World Series. The Indians won the pennant again in 1954, but lost to the New York Giants in the series.

Under head coach Paul E. Brown, the Cleveland Browns won every All-American Football Conference championship between 1946 and 1949. When the team joined the National Football League in 1950, they dispelled any criticism by defeating the Los Angeles Rams for the NFL championship. Although the retirement of quarterback Otto Graham in 1956 gave the Browns their first losing season, the drafting of running back Jim Brown in

1957 revitalized the offense. Jim Brown's stellar performance put Cleveland back on the winning track. By 1964, the Browns with Blanton Collier as head coach reclaimed the NFL championship. Although Jim Brown's jersey was retired, he did not. After a motion picture career, he returned to the Browns as a special consultant in 1993.

When Cleveland's war-time mayor Frank Lausche was elected governor in 1945, he passed the gauntlet of city leadership to his law director Thomas A. Burke. Burke transformed the city's transportation system extending the rapid transit system from the Terminal complex westward to the Cleveland-Hopkins International Airport. Further, his commitment to building a downtown airport to relieve overcrowding at Hopkins led to the construction of the lakefront airport that now bears his name. Under Burke's administration, Cleveland became a national leader in ending discrimination when the city established the Community Relations Board. This action was reinforced when the city council passed one of the nations first Civil Right Act in 1946.

Another unrelated civil rights movement was also beginning in Cleveland, the birth of rock 'n' roll. Allen Freed, a local disc jockey began to introduce rhythm 'n' blues to white audiences and white performers. Rock 'n' roll is a combination of blues and rhythm 'n' blues (no jack, Mack, I can't take the hack, even with sound this don't rebound). After the Second World War, Freed began playing rhythm 'n' blues for Akron listeners at WAKR before moving across the radio dial to Cleveland's WJW in 1951. To popularize this music to all listeners, Freed joined Leo Mintz a local record retailer, to develop the phrase "rock 'n' roll." In Cleveland, Allen Freed, known as "Moon Dog" to his listeners, generated an enormous interracial following. Freed's crowning achievement came in March 1952, when he sponsored the nation's first rock concert, the "Moon Dog Coronation Ball," where an audience of over 25,000 black and white participants came to the Cleveland Arena and witnessed the birth of rock 'n' roll.

Burke also moved against policy operations and police corruption. Additionally, he successfully campaigned for a charter amendment to permit the mayor to appoint and remove the police chief. A former racket breaking assistant county prosecutor in the 1930's, Burke served as mayor until he was appointed by Governor Lausche to fill an unexpired term in the U.S. Senate in 1953.

Burke's successor Anthony J. Celebrezze, a democratic State Senator, ran as an independent Democrat against the party favorite, County Engineer Albert Porter. Supported by Burke,

Governor Lausche and the editor of the *Cleveland Press*, Louis Seltzer, Celebrezze easily defeated Porter.

Celebrezze entered the mayor's office with a vision of Cleveland, with middle class homes mushrooming from poor inner city neighborhoods and the flowering of a new downtown. As mayor, he launched the county's largest effort at urban renewal. Unable to secure private developers for his grandiose home-building plans, his actions ultimately aggravated the city's housing shortages.

The mayor was more successful in his determination to change the focus of downtown development toward Lake Erie. Although the conservative Cleveland banking interests originally shied away from Erieview, a Columbus developer John W. Galbreath was willing to gamble on the project. Galbreath's 40 story Erieview Tower, designed by I.M. Pei and Associates, served as the anchor for a dozen structures which followed over the next two decades. Cyrus Eaton who had been instrumental in making Cleveland Trust the largest bank in Cleveland was infuriated by the lack of commitment by the city's financial leaders. Employing Carl Stokes as his attorney, Eaton instituted legal proceedings against Cleveland Trust to embarrass the banking giant into investing "risk capital" in the city.

Celebrezze secured an $8 million bond to promote the port authority and Cleveland as a world trade center in preparation for the opening of the St. Lawrence Seaway in 1959. His highly popular low tax philosophy led to reduced services for city residents as many former city services were taken over by the county including the Blossom Hill School for Girls, the City Hospital (Metro-General) and the Hudson Boy's Farm. Clevelanders overwhelmingly supported Celebrezze's actions, as he won an unprecedented fifth term as chief executive capturing every ward in the city and garnishing nearly 74 percent of the popular vote. With enrollment up by a third, and one of ten on a half day schedule, voters also enthusiastically approved a bond issued to build more schools, indicating the confidence that the electorate felt in Celebrezze. In 1962, Celebrezze resigned to serve as President Kennedy's Secretary of Health, Education and Welfare.

SUGGESTIONS FOR READING

Richard G. Forbis, "Eastern North America," and Paul Tolstoy, "From the Old World to the New World Via The Bering Strait," *North America* (1975), are dated but there is little written on the Hopewell. Jare R. Cardinal and Eric J. Cardinal, "Archaeology and History: Some Suggestions from the Historians Viewpoint," and Phillip R. Shriver, "The Beaver War's and the Destruction of the Erie Nation," *Ohio's Western Reserve A Regional Reader* (1988), are top of the line on the demise of Erie Indians.

Thomas Jefferson's, *Notes on the State of Virginia*, 1787 (1955), provides a unique insight into pre-constitution thought as well as a good description of Lord Dunmore's War. Gordon S. Wood, *The Creation of the American Republic 1776—1787* (1969), offers an excellent history of American under the Articles of Confederation.

George J. Barmann and Todd Simon, *Cleveland a City Grows to Greatness* (1962), presents a generally rosy overview of the city's history. Thomas F. Campbell and Edward M. Miggins, ed., *The Birth of Modern Cleveland 1865—1930* (1988), presents a good rendition of the problems associated with industrialization. Three essays are outstanding, Campbell's, "Mounting Crisis and Reform Cleveland's Political Development," Miggins and Mary Morgenthaler, "The Settlement of Cleveland by the New Immigrants and Migrants," and Darwin H. Stapleton, "The City Industrious: How Technology Transformed Cleveland." George C. Condon, *Cleveland, the Best Kept Secret* (1981), a fun book, insightful. John J. Grabowski and David D. Van Tassel, ed., *The Encyclopedia of Cleveland History* (1987), offers such a wealth of knowledge on the city that it is difficult to adequately describe. Moreover, the introductory historical overview by the editors, "Toward the Postindustrial City: 1930—1980," Ronald Weiner, "The New Industrial Metropolis: 1860—1929," and Robert Wheeler, "A Commercial Hamlet is Founded 1796—1824," are spectacular. A collateral work by Carol Poh Miller and Robert Wheeler, *Cleveland A Concise History, 1796—1990* (1990), presents a fine history of Cleveland, and it's reasonably priced. William Ganson Rose, *Cleveland the Making of a City* (1990), is excellent. Rose uses overviews and year by year accounts to give the reader a detailed history of Cleveland through the Second World War. This work is first rate.

PART II

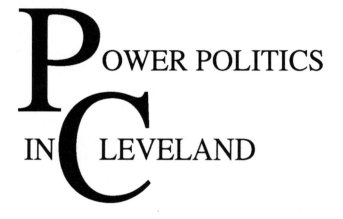

POWER POLITICS IN CLEVELAND

A CITY IN DECLINE

Cleveland's mayor Anthony Celebrezze's innovative approach to urban problems won him national attention and a cabinet position from President Kennedy. However, Celebrezze's programs accelerated the forces already at work challenging urban America. It was left to his successor, Ralph Locher, to deal with the consequences of these actions which fundamentally altered the social, economic and political configuration of the City of Cleveland.

Ralph Locher had previously served as executive secretary for Governor Lausche, and as Celebrezze's law director. As the city's legal representative, Locher earned political credentials by testifying against utility rate increases in the Ohio General Assembly and by his enforcement of the city's anti-discrimination laws. After being appointed mayor, Locher successfully mediated a minority hiring dispute between Plumbers Local #55 and the United Freedom Movement, an umbrella civil rights organization, thereby averting picketing at municipal building projects. These endeavors and his ethnic heritage enabled him to easily win the 1963 mayoral election.

Although Cleveland voters at times approved of an unendorsed Democrat like Celebrezze, the city remained essentially Democratic. This trend evolved during the presidency of Franklin D. Roosevelt and the New Deal programs established by his administration. Because of these national policies, a political alliance was forged between the white ethnic and black communities making possible the creation of a single party rule. But the continual victories of the Democratic Party tended to weaken its perception of the problems facing the city. These problems became increasingly evident during the early 1960's when the coalition proceeded to benefit the cosmos far more than black Clevelanders. The city government became entrenched in a political leadership which proved unable to deal effectively with the problems facing the city. Thus Cleveland, faced with the same or similar metropolitan problems as other urban areas, was handicapped because it had neither viable alternative programs, initiated by an effective opposition party nor an efficient administration able to bring forth meaningful reforms.

This type of political system also encouraged special interest groups to maintain their own economic and political control by manipulating change so as not to fundamentally alter

the continuation of the status quo. Ralph S. Locher's first administration merely reflected the decline of the city. As mayor of Cleveland, Locher a man of honesty and integrity, lacked the ability to
move decisively to stem the deterioration of the city. Yet his
actions did not threaten either the position or the authority of the
business interests in Cleveland. His programs, no matter how well
publicized, typically failed to materialize as Cleveland became a
city of ideas without implementation and tended to look at past
accomplishments rather than face the prevailing situation. What
Cleveland needed was a total reformation; what she acquired was
political stagnation, easily controllable by special interests.

Already reeling from the loss of businesses and homes
caused by the Interstate Highway Program and the expansion of
the airport, Locher inherited his predecessor's massive intercity
slum clearance effort which failed to attract commitments or
investments by local developers and banking interests. Almost
totally dependent upon property tax revenues, the city as well as
the public school system suffered irreparable fiscal losses as a
result of declining taxable assets. Worse, Clevelanders continued
to accept Celebrezze's low tax philosophy, as voters defeated
Locher's attempt to initiate an income tax in 1965. His inability to
convince residents of the necessity of raising revenues would
push the city to the brink of anarchy by 1966.

Cleveland's housing crisis had reached the acute stage.
The city's urban renewal effort had eradicated thousands of lower
income homes without providing alternative residential housing
as racism, blockbusting and white flight contributed to hostility,
instability and an ever increasing exodus of whites to the suburbs.
Between 1960 and 1970, the total number of housing units in the
city declined by over 6.7 percent (note Table 4).

In addition, employment opportunities also moved from
the central core to the surrounding suburbs. Increasingly, suburbs
began to attract higher paying manufacturing enterprises, inexpensive suburban sites were ideal locations for the large scale
factory units constructed following the Second World War. By the
early Fifties, Chevrolet opened a transmission plant in Parma,
while Ford built a stamping plant in Walton Hills and an engine
plant in Brook Park. Urban renewal projects, racial tensions and
redlining (a conscious and deliberate pattern of rejecting loan
applications and/or coverage by local banks and insurance companies to selective central city neighborhoods) continued to drain
jobs from the central city. Furthermore, as area retail stores migrated to the suburbs, they became less concerned with their more
marginal downtown operations.

Employing a farebox mentality, the Cleveland Transit System (CTS) failed to follow their former patrons along the concrete interstate ribbons to suburbia. Cleveland's suburbs were forced to become more dependent upon automobiles than other metropolitan areas because CTS ignored the emerging population growth patterns. Instead, declining ridership led to ever-increasing fares and reduced services as the inadequate public transportation system and the lack of parking facilities, combined with the city's emphasis upon Erieview, contributed to an overall decline in the downtown area. By the end of the 1960's, three of the six major downtown retail operations had closed, and many of the theaters including the Allen, Ohio, Palace and State Theaters, along Playhouse Square followed suit.

By 1967, CTS had become such a liability for Cleveland that the city was forced to use general operating funds to keep the transit system services operating at a minimal level. Unable to generate enough revenues to receive noticeable matching federal gas tax funds, CTS was merged with suburban bus lines into a Regional Transit Authority (RTA) in 1975. Financed by a one percent sales tax, RTA was able to modernize public transit within the county.

In the long run Erieview brought about a positive transformation for Cleveland by promoting the service sector. Celebrezze's vision helped to keep the Forest City competitive in the 1980's and the 1990's. However, in the 1960's and the 1970's, Cleveland's civic leaders viewed the city as an industrial and manufacturing center and criticized the project for diverting attention away from the downtown area. Locher was unable to overcome intransigence which continued to thwart the project during his tenure.

During the 60's, suburbs grew at the expense of the city of Cleveland, Cuyahoga County's population increased by over 4 percent and the Standard Metropolitan Statistical Area (SMSA) expanded by 13 percent between 1960 and 1970, during the same period, Cleveland witnessed a 14 percent decline in city residents. This migration to suburbia would profoundly affect the political structure of the central city. Although the number of African Americans increased only by 37,000 in the 60's as compared to over 100,000 during the previous decade, Cleveland's white population declined by nearly 165,000 in the 1960's. Overall, the percentage of blacks in the Forest City moved from 28.6 percent in 1960, to 38.3 percent of the total population in 1970 (see SMSA/PMSA table number 9) and as the percentage of blacks increased, so did their political strength.

However, traditional hiring patterns by employers and

unions prevented any noticeable change in employment prospects for African Americans. Cleveland, once a national leader in promoting civil rights, became the perpetrator of institutional racism by failing to add blacks and other minorities to meaningful positions, particularly within the city's police department.

Moreover, the mayor supported Superintendent Paul Briggs' and the school board's ill-fated decision to build new facilities in overcrowded black neighborhoods rather than desegregate under-utilized white schools. Despite protests and increasing acts of violence, Locher continued to back the superintendent and the board who insisted that they were supporting neighborhood schools by their actions, whereas opponents argued that many of the schools could just as easily be constructed where both races could attend integrated facilities.

Growing charges of discrimination and unequal law enforcement by Cleveland's liberal white and black communities were ignored by the Locher administration. During the mayor's first full term, this type of unresponsive behavior was characterized by the administration's refusal to halt the process of de facto school segregation by the Board of Education or even attempt to converse with those individuals protesting the Board's policies. Locher's inaction witnessed violent clashes between the segregated Italian neighborhood of Murray Hill and the United Freedom Movement, a coalition civil rights organizations seeking to promote unified action in the fields of employment, housing and education. Incidents such as the stoning of black school children and the attack on United Freedom Movement pickets by residents of Murray Hill provoked even broader responses by the Civil Rights Organization.

Subsequent sit-ins, a school boycott by black students and the death of the Western Reserve University campus minister, Rev. Bruce Klunder who was killed while protesting the construction of yet another segregated school, were all unable to stop the continuation of segregation. When members of the United Freedom Movement attempted to talk to the mayor, they were refused admission after the city's chief executive stated that they could not "shoot their way into his office."[1] The *Plain Dealer*, basically implied that such actions were communist inspired and the *Cleveland Press*, which was under the personal domain of Louis B. Seltzer, urged "responsible Negro Leaders" to mediate the situation. Although some of Locher's previous actions in dealing with the United Freedom Movement had initiated negative editorial responses, he was still able to count on the overall support of influential corporate executives and the local media.[2]

In 1965 Carl Stokes launched a dynamic campaign to unseat Locher as mayor. Stokes had been elected as the state's first black Democrat to the Ohio House of Representatives in 1962. Carl Stokes, a former assistant city prosecutor and a Democratic representative in the General Assembly, ran as an independent in 1965 hoping to win the mayors office in a three-way race.

During the 1965 campaign, despite the vacillation of the city and the Mayor's ineffective leadership, Locher continued to have the support of the business and ethnic communities and the endorsement of the city's two major newspapers, the *Cleveland Press* and the *Plain Dealer*. Typical of this journalistic support for Ralph Locher, the *Plain Dealer* accused the *Call and Post*, Cleveland's major black newspaper, of issuing "rotten racist propaganda" when the *Post* advocated such opinions as "the Negro who votes against Stokes is a traitor" and "the Negro who cowardly stays home to keep from voting is worse." Yet in the same editorial response, the *Plain Dealer* stated: "Taken as a rule of conduct, that would mean any white man or woman would be a traitor to his group if he voted for Stokes." In case there was any doubt as to the intention of the opinion expressed by the *Plain Dealer*, the editorial concluded with these remarks:

> Our trust is in the voter's common sense
> and fairness. We believe he is hard to fool, collec-
> tively. He will, we believe, go out Tuesday and do
> the honest, common-sense job at the polls and
> re-elect Mayor Ralph S. Locher.[3]

Locher's political strength stemmed from his Romanian heritage and political philosophy: "Conservative and patriotic, Locher was the ideal public servant to sell to the ethnic community."[4] Further, the relationship between the white ethnic and the Negro components within the City was potentially antagonistic:

> . . . the Cleveland social milieu is complicated
> further by the existence of closely knit white ethnic
> groups, many of which hold strong antipathies
> toward outsiders and especially toward Negroes.
> This situation presents points of conflict that are
> potentially explosive; it also poses an obstacle to
> coordinated efforts on the part of the community
> and its local government (especially the City of
> Cleveland) to ameliorate social distress.[5]

Carl Stokes' strategy in his unsuccessful bid for mayor in the 1965 election was to run as an independent, create an alliance between black and liberal white voters, and hope that the remaining white vote would split between the Democratic and Republican candidates in the general election. Of the 236,577 votes cast, he lost by only 2500 votes.[6] Locher's subsequent re-election after a recount merely hastened the problems facing the city.

The Cleveland establishment responds only if it is threatened by violence (whether actual or potential) or the national media, or if it feels its proposals are ignored or its authority is questioned. Two events during the mayor's tenure eroded the establishment's support and ultimately provoked their wrath. The first event occurred on June 7, 1965, when Cleveland's police chief, Richard Wagner, testified in defense of capital punishment before an Ohio House Committee in Columbus. Wagner justified his position by stating: "We have people saying they intend to overthrow the government of the United States and, incidentally, shoot all the Caucasians. One of these groups is RAM." The implication that a Cleveland organization, the Revolutionary Action Movement, was subversive, outraged the liberal and black communities.[7]

Secondly, a violent racially inspired upheaval in the predominately black neighborhood of Hough converted a fear of confrontation into a reality in July 1966. Random acts of arson, looting, and violence irrupted after a confrontation between the police and Hough residents leaving four dead and about thirty injured between July 18-24, 1966. Realizing the fears of the business community, Locher called in the National Guard and initiated a grand jury probe into the causes of the incident.

The Grand Jury and its foreman, Louis B. Seltzer, labeled the conflict a "riot" which had been "precipitated and exploited" by a "small group of trained and disciplined professionals" including specific members of the JFK House, the W.E.B. DuBois Club, outside agitators and the Communist Party of Ohio. Further, Locher's insistence, before Senator Ribicoff's subcommittee hearings, that the incidents in Hough were Communist inspired brought the administration's failures to the national media, since the two Cleveland policemen who had infiltrated the Communist Party of Ohio responded that there was no connection between the, party's activities and Hough. A subsequent inquiry by the Cleveland Citizens Committee on the Hough Disturbances found that the incidents in Hough were spontaneous and uncoordinated. Furthermore, the citizens hearing criticized the Grand Jury for its direct violation of the Ohio Code by mentioning names of people without sufficient evidence to indict them and for "commending the police force which the panel found in need of a better community relationship."[8]

Locher's administration came increasingly under the scrutiny of the local news media as well, following the Hough incident. On July 25, 1966, the *Cleveland Press* in an editorial entitled "Peace is Raging" exposed some of the actions taken by the mayor which indicated the irresponsible behavior of the administration:

About six weeks ago, Mayor Locher met in Washington with Secretary Robert Weaver of the Housing and Urban Development Department. Secretary Weaver gave the mayor a list of the city's responsibilities for its stagnating East Side. Things about housing, derelict buildings, parking, playgrounds, garbage and so on. Because the mayor failed to act on recommended playgrounds for Hough and Garden Valley, Cleveland last week lost a federal grant of $1,500,000 for parks and playgrounds.[9] By December 1966, the *Plain Dealer*, in an editorial entitled "Inertia at City Hall," attacked the mayor openly. The article began with the question "What is Wrong at Cleveland's City Hall?" And it responded:

Inertia.
Bumbling administration.
Lack of foresight, of imagination and vision.
This is what knowledgeable people have been
saying for many months. This is what not only
politicians, but also businessmen and others who
have come away from City Hall baffled and frus-
trated have been saying.[10]

Earlier, the mayor had supported the business-established Little Hoover Commission, which was to investigate and recommend improvements on the operations of the city government. When the commission's final report criticized the administration, especially in the areas of urban renewal, police reform and inter-departmental cooperation, Locher accused the businessmen of being politically motivated in their report and he refused to implement many of their recommendations. Cleveland lost an additional $10 million in federal urban renewal aid because of disorganized program that Locher had instituted.[11] Despite the $10 million federal warning, the mayor ignored the proposed changes suggested by the Little Hover Commission and refused to noticeably improve the city's urban renewal program. Disgusted with Locher's lack of progress, the department of Housing and Urban Development (HUD) froze all urban renewal funds to the city. Locher's actions succeeded in alienating Cleveland's business community from any further involvement with his administration.

Table 6: Cleveland's Population
1900-1990

Year		Population
1900	———	381.768
1910	———	560,663
1920	———	786,841
1930	———	900,429
1940	———	878,336
1950	———	914,808
1960	———	876,050
1970	———	750,879
1980	———	573,822
1990	———	505,616

Source: Census Bureau

References

[1]Estelle Zannes, *Checkmate in Cleveland: The Rhetoric of Confrontation During the Stokes Years* (Cleveland, 1972) pp. 9-28.

Referring to the success of the school boycott, Zannes' found that the display of massive unity was generally not sustained mainly because of the ideological conflict within the black community over separation and integration philosophies. Similarly this is one of the problems that Harold Cruse, *The Crisis of the Negro Intellectual* (New York, 1969) would find restraining the black community from a unified action, pp. 245-264.

For an excellent general overview of Cleveland's politics during this era see John J. Grabowski and David D. Van Tassel, "Toward the Post-industrial City: 1930 -1980," *The Encyclopedia of Cleveland History* (Cleveland, 1987). pp. xliii-lv.

[2]*Plain Dealer*, February 5, 1964, *Cleveland Press*, April 14, 1964, and Zannes, p. 28.

[3]*Plain Dealer*, October 29, 1965.

The role that Cleveland newspapers play in determining mayoral candidates in the city is immense. Even Edward C. Banfield's and James Q. Wilson's *City Politics*, which presents a scholarly confrontation to some of the views expressed in this work, cites the political strength of the two Cleveland dailies:

> It (Cleveland) has a party organization (Democratic) but, a declining one. Its newspapers, the *Press* and the *Plain Dealer* (particularly the former) have elected mayors for about a quarter of a century with little help from the party and sometimes over its opposition. The mayors of Cleveland accordingly have been . . . good-government types, whereas the city councilmen, who have been chosen by the party and not the newspapers have been politicians of the old school.

See Edward C. Banfield and James Q. Wilson, *City Politics* (Cambridge, Massachusetts, 1966) p. 325.

[4]Carl B. Stokes, *Promises of Power: A Political Autobiography* (New York, 1973) p. 80.

In Andrew Greeley's "The Alienation of White Ethnic Groups," Greeley presents both the conservative nature of the ethnic community and perhaps an intriguing explanation of Ralph Perk's appeal to Cleveland's ethnic voters:

> Finally, the ethnics find themselves increas-
> ingly isolated from their own political leadership.
> In cities like Chicago where patronage and a pre-
> cinct organization still maintain some sort of
> communication between the grass roots and the
> city hall, the problem is less acute than it is in cities
> where so-called "good government" has cut the
> liberal elites who run the city off from the ethnic
> hinterlands. But even in cities where ethnic politics
> is still a way of life, the alienation of white ethnics
> from their leadership is growing more intense.

See Andrew Greeley, "The Alienation of White Ethnic Groups,"
Why Can't They Be Like Us (New York, 1969) p. 163.

However, in the tables presented in Greeley's later work,
Ethnicity in the United States, he found the ethnic community much
more liberal than Protestants of Western European origins. See
Andrew Greeley, *Ethnicity in the United States: A Preliminary
Reconnaissance* (New York, 1974) Table 3.

[5]Frederick Stocker, "Fiscal Disparities in Cleveland, Ohio,"
Advisory Commission on Inter-Government Relations (October,
1967) p. 252.

In addition, Thomas F. Pettigrew found that in 1967 and in
1969 ethnic Clevelanders were most likely to vote against Stokes
and in the National election for Wallace:

> But in the Ohio City (Cleveland) our expec-
> tations were verified, that is, Polish Americans,
> Hungarian Americans, Czech Americans, and so
> forth, were most likely to vote against Stokes and
> for Wallace in neighborhoods which were largely
> ethnic enclaves for one group.

See Thomas F. Pettigrew, "When a Black Candidate Runs for
Mayor: Race and Voting Behavior," in Harlan Hahn, *People and
Politics in Urban Society* (Beverly Hills, 1972) p. 101.

Cleveland's Hungarian newspaper *Szabadsag* supported
Carl Stokes for mayor.

[6]Ralph W. Conant and Alan Shank, *Urban Perspectives:
Politics and Policies* (Boston, 1975) pp. 199-200.

[7]Zannes, pp. 30-31.

[8]Report relating to the Hough Riot, The Cuyahoga County
Grand Jury, Louis B. Seltzer, Grand Jury Foremen, August 1966,
Grabowski and Van Tassel, pp. li-lii, 521, and Zannes, pp. 4-28.

[9]*Cleveland Press*, July 25, 1966.

[10]*Plain Dealer*, December 12, 1966.

[11]Kenneth G. Weinberg, *Black Victory: Carl Stokes and the Winning of Cleveland* (Chicago, 1968) p. 71, and Stokes, p. 95.

THE CLEVELAND OCTOPUS

Read the history of Tom Loftin Johnson, the
man now revered as the greatest mayor in the
history of Cleveland, and learn what happens
when you fight the power structure. A wealthy
man when he came into office in 1901, he is praised
today for what he achieved, but few remember he
was defeated for re-election, broken financially and
physically. He died less than a year after he left
office, disowned by the establishment from which
he had come. He fought both of the political parties
and was at sword's point with the newspapers of
his day for almost the entire eight years he was in
office. Looking at his career, you have to realize
that whenever you go against the established
structure, it is going to be self-destructive. It happened to Carl Stokes between 1967 and 1971, but it
also happened to a wealthy white man over fifty
years ago.

Carl B. Stokes, *Promises of Power: A Political
Autobiography*, p, 226.

Carl Stokes, as a Cleveland attorney, did not fully comprehend the Cleveland power structure. Perhaps the reason for his
distorted view was due to his relationship with Cyrus Eaton.
Eaton's rise to economic prominence in Cleveland before the crash
of 1929 and his subsequent losses during the 1930's hurt many
Cleveland establishment figures who had invested heavily in his
holdings. Moreover, Eaton's tremendous recovery following the
depression angered many of those financially weakened because
of their earlier relations with the multi-millionaire. For this reason,
Eaton's wealth forced him to be a part of the business community-
but in reality, he remained aloof from the establishment.

Thus, when an outsider Cyrus Eaton brought suit against
George Gund, the chief executive of the powerful Cleveland Trust
Company, using Carl Stokes as his attorney, it was not the inter-
establishment conflict that Stokes perceived. Eaton instituted legal
proceedings to convince the banking giant to invest in Cleveland.
Cleveland Trust had steadfastly refused to invest risk capital in
the city, instead the bank continued to invest in her traditional
manufacturing and industrial clients. Carl Stokes understood the

personal nature of the dispute,[1] but not Eaton's peculiar relationship within the city's business community.

Much of George Gund's personal wealth was created by
purchasing blue chip stocks at bargain basement "Bailey prices"
during the depression. However, Gund's power in Cleveland
stemmed from his service on over thirty corporate boards as
president or chairman of the city's largest bank, Cleveland Trust.
In addition, Gund served on over a dozen boards involved in
civic, cultural, educational and philanthropic endeavors. In 1952,
he established the George Gund Foundation which continues to
award grants for a wide assortment of artistic, community, economic and environmental concerns. By April 1994 over $200
million had been donated through his foresight and generosity.[2]

Cleveland Trust, renamed AmeriTrust during the Kucinich
era, was accused but not indicted by banking regulators of favorit-
ism in granting loans to selective tool and die companies in the
60's. During this era the city's largest bank even maintained a
controlling interest in the *Plain Dealer*. The power of Cleveland
banks can be seen when two *Fortune* 500 companies attempted to
vacate the area; Cleveland banks forced in the collapse of
Addressograph-Multigraph (AM International) in California and
White Motors in Michigan by demanding immediate repayment
of short term loans.

Today the Forest City's major corporate, banking, and
legal firms are members of the board of trustees for the Greater
Cleveland Growth Association, Cleveland Tomorrow. The CEO's
of these business establishments routinely serve as trustees on the
community's business, civic, cultural, educational, and philanthropic boards.[3]

When Cyrus Eaton similarly served as a trustee on numerous boards his position remained one of an outsider, an
anti-establishment figure. The name of Cyrus Eaton was awesome; it conjured up bad memories in the minds of the business
community, and Carl Stokes used this name almost as a club to
win recognition by businessmen. For example, after his election to
the Ohio House of Representatives in 1962, Stokes was told he
could serve on any committee he wished except banking, because
of his relationship with Cyrus Eaton.[4]

Two trends evolved during Carl Stokes' tenure as an Ohio
legislator. First, he sponsored and supported legislation for the
black community, especially in the field of fair housing. Also, in
defiance of the Democratic leadership, he supported the Republican Governor, James Rhodes' proposed electoral changes follow-

ing the one-man, one-vote decision of the U.S. Supreme Court, enabling more black legislators to serve the state. Legislatively under-represented for decades in the General Assembly, Cuyahoga County also became recognized as part of the State of Ohio in 1967, by establishing the principal that legislatures should represent people not acres. The Federal Court decisions in *Baker v Carr* (1962) and *Reynolds v Sims* (1964) mandated that Cuyahoga County with one ninth of the states population be correspondingly represented in the General Assembly. The second trend, becoming more pronounced after 1965, was closely allied with the Cleveland business community when Stokes co-sponsored an anti-riot bill which permitted the rapid mobilization of the National Guard to deal with urban unrest and "began to talk a great deal about law and order in the streets."[5]

These establishment links were not formalized by the 1965 primary and although strongly supported by the civil rights organizations and the black community still feeling the unity of the school boycott, Stokes lost the election. Yet the significance of this loss may have been more important than the Ohio legislator realized. As the Reverend Charles Rawlings stated: "I am very sorry it did not happen in 1965 because, if it had, the liberal community could have owned Stokes. It happened in 1967, and the business community owns him."[6]

After his defeat, Carl Stokes applied pressure to his former client and the city's business community. When interviewed for a *Cleveland Press* series on corporate involvement in urban affairs, he stated: "We have not had a business leader with enough security of his own and with a modern concept of government to sell the rest of the business community on why it is important to make Cleveland a thriving community, not only for prestige but for a wider tax base and higher employment."[7] With the election of 1967 on the horizon, Carl Stokes hired Eaton's public relations man for the campaign, and it was later charged and not denied that Eaton paid his fee.[8] Once again, Carl Stokes failed to perceive the establishment in its true form. His remained a distorted view of the establishment, which was predicated upon the belief that he could control the business elite by using the counter resources of the iron master. The fallacy of the policy rested in the legislator's contention that Eaton was an integral part of the establishment.

The establishment's power extended into nearly every area of cultural, educational and financial life in the city. Exerting control through a complex network of interdependent councils, commissions, and foundations, Cleveland executives wove a web of control over the area. These business creations acted like the tentacles of an octopus to restrain opponents, retain order and preserve the interests of the establishment. Moreover, like the octopus, the business community utilized it's own type of secretion to avoid detection-the press.

Confronted by the racial problems facing the Cleveland Public School System, business leaders reacted by forming the Businessmen's Interracial Committee. These corporate executives were instrumental in bringing Paul Briggs, then superintendent of Parma Public Schools, to head the Cleveland system. Once Briggs became the superintendent of the Cleveland Public Schools, the Businessmen Interracial Committee proceeded to work closely with him to formulate both public statements and plans for the system. Moreover, the Businessmen's Interracial Committee lobbied for Ohio's Fair Housing Law and encouraged area banks and savings and loan associations to make non-discriminatory mortgage loans to blacks. Financially, the committee derived its funds from the Cleveland and the Ford Foundations.[9]

In the area of cultural and civic improvements, chief executives served on the boards and directed the processes which affected the city by dominating the boards of trustees of the Cleveland Art Museum, the Cleveland Ballet (founded in the early 1970's), the Cleveland Health Museum, the Cleveland Natural History Museum, the Cleveland Opera Association, the Cleveland Play House, Case Western Reserve University, Cleveland State University, and United Way. Urban renewal projects and the redevelopment of such areas as University Circle, downtown and Cleveland State University were largely in the hands of the establishment through its control of the University Circle Development Foundation and the Cleveland Development Foundation. Furthermore, business leaders played a major roll in the founding of Cleveland State University and Cuyahoga Community College.[10]

Following the Hough disorders, the business community founded the Inner City Action Committee. Ralph Besse, the chairman of the Cleveland Electric Illuminating Company, directed the committee's activities, which included working closely with the Businessmen's Interracial Committee. By February 1967, the Inner City Action Committee openly attacked Locher for his ineffective urban renewal program. An additional reason for this attack was Locher's rejection of important elements of the Little Hoover Commission's final report which was greatly financed by the Cleveland Foundation. Furthermore, Besse's committee amassed a private fund of $40,000 to pay militant black leaders to keep the city calm, this project was directed by Baxter Hill.[11]

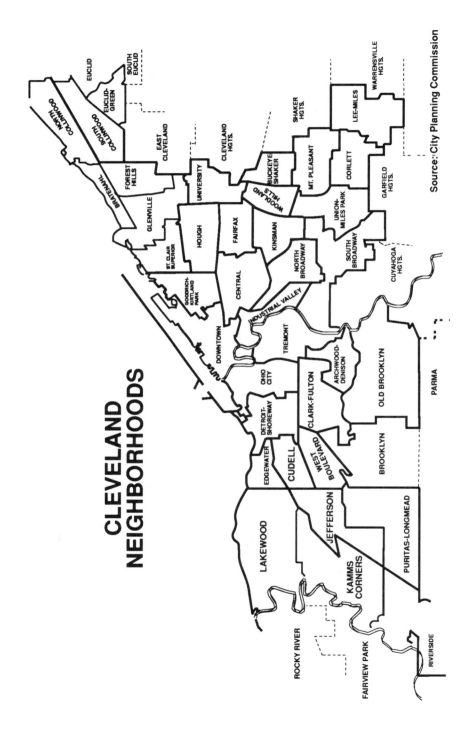

CLEVELAND
NEIGHBORHOODS

Source: City Planning Commission

EUCLID

SOUTH EUCLID

EUCLID-GREEN

WARRENSVILLE HGTS.

SHAKER HGTS.

LEE-MILES

NORTH COLLINWOOD

SOUTH COLLINWOOD

EAST CLEVELAND

CLEVELAND HGTS.

BUCKEYE SHAKER

MT. PLEASANT

CORLETT

BRATENAHL

FOREST HILLS

UNIVERSITY

WOODLAND HILLS

GARFIELD HGTS.

GLENVILLE

HOUGH

FAIRFAX

KINSMAN

UNION-MILES PARK

ST. CLAIR SUPERIOR

CENTRAL

NORTH BROADWAY

SOUTH BROADWAY

CUYAHOGA HGTS.

GOODRICH-KIRTLAND PARK

INDUSTRIAL VALLEY

DOWNTOWN

TREMONT

OHIO CITY

ARCHWOOD-DENISON

OLD BROOKLYN

PARMA

DETROIT-SHOREWAY

CLARK-FULTON

EDGEWATER

CUDELL

WEST BOULEVARD

BROOKLYN

LAKEWOOD

JEFFERSON

PURITAS-LONGMEAD

KAMMS CORNERS

ROCKY RIVER

FAIRVIEW PARK

RIVERSIDE

The establishment emerged following the Hough conflict, united in their opposition of Locher. Disillusioned with Locher, their immediate inclination was to support the political aspirations of Frank Celeste, the former mayor of the Cleveland suburb of Lakewood, who had announced his candidacy early in the 1967 primary.[12] However, following the lead of the Ford Foundation, the momentum turned to Carl B. Stokes. The Ford Foundation feared that racial unrest would inevitably result without a fundamental change at City Hall. What the organization's President McGeorge Bundy feared was that: "the white man's companies (would have) to take the losses."[13] Thus, the Ford Foundation sought to promote voter registration as an alternative to violence, thereby enhancing stability and testing a black mayoral candidate's ability to quiet the inner city.

Actions taken by the Ford Foundation to encourage voter registration in Cleveland included: a $175,000 grant to the Congress of Racial Equality, and a $250,000 grant to the Southern Christian Leadership Conference, of which $27,899.40 was used in the Cleveland drive. The Businessmen's Interracial Committee also presented a $5,000 check to Dr. Martin Luther King Jr. for voter registration. The implications behind the Foundation's actions were clearly evident after the Government Research Institute's findings were released in 1965, indicating the potential political might of the black community in Cleveland. Coincidentally, the Institute was a fact-finding group of the Citizens League, a body substantially controlled by Cleveland corporate executives.[14]

By 1967, the objectives of the establishment were fulfilled and their goals of removing Locher, controlling racial unrest, and instituting a black mayor were completed. Supported by the tentacles of the octopus, the Stokes victory in the Democratic primary and general election obviously came as no surprise to the business community. Stokes was endorsed by both major newspapers in the primary, which meant leading all opposition candidates in news coverage as well in Cleveland. The overall success of this program was presented by Whitney Young, Jr., the director of the Urban League, who stated that: "Cleveland Negroes did not riot last summer (1967) because they anticipated a reward that Carl Stokes would be elected mayor." Further, Leo Jackson, a highly respected black councilman, declared that the business community was buying security in 1967 in the form of a black mayor.[15]

National fame and notoriety preceded and followed the mayoral victory of Carl Stokes. The national media responded favorably to the mayor, making him the subject of numerous journal and periodical articles and television broadcasts. In addition the Cleveland mayor, was awarded the Horatio Alger Award by the American Schools and Colleges Association. Moreover, a Harris poll of black men and women indicated that Carl Stokes was the most highly respected black public official in the nation.[16]

A more productive relationship also emerged on the state government level, between the conservative state house and the Democratic city, because of the previous rapport established between the former legislator and Governor Rhodes. On the federal level, the Johnson administration also found it politically pleasing to have a black mayor in a major metropolitan area during the upcoming 1968 presidential election.

Stokes convinced HUD officials to release the urban renewal funds impounded during Locher's tenure and launched an ambitious revitalization program called Cleveland: NOW!. Cleveland: NOW! was envisioned to create community, health and youth centers, employment opportunities, housing, and to expand Erieview into Erieview II. Corporate sponsorships and individual donations were combined with city and state revenues to obtain federal matching funds. Stokes persuaded the city council to increase the city income tax from one half to one percent to help fund Cleveland: NOW! and the business community rallied behind the mayor and avidly supported his program until a July evening in 1968.

During the summer of 1968, additional funds were spent to keep Cleveland quiet by the Ford Foundation in an attempt to manipulate the militants within the city.[17] However, a reassessment of the terms of the insurance policy began when Cleveland's black mayor was photographed with black militants, followed two days later with the Glenville shootings. On July 23, 1968, a well-armed group of black militants confronted Cleveland police in a blaze of gunfire that resulted in seven deaths (three policemen, three suspects and one civilian). Mayor Stokes requested and received assistance by the Ohio National Guard to stop random acts of arson and looting after the Glenville shoot-out. Although the mayor's responses led to the rapid restoration of order, the business community once again became fearful.

Negative disclosures by the press became more pronounced, as Stokes would later write: "Glenville came like the cutting of a leash." When it was uncovered that money allocated for Cleveland: NOW! had been given to Fred "Ahmed" Evans, the black militant accused of engineering the shoot-out, the mayor's popularity suffered greatly, as Stokes described it: "Glenville killed much of my public support." Alienated by the Glenville incident, the business community opted out of Cleveland: NOW!, which operated on a matching fund basis. As Stokes later wrote: "Many businessmen who had made pledges to the Cleveland: NOW! program, quietly turned their backs, and we could see there would be no support for its continuance. The overall mood of distrust was devastating."[18]

Despite the Glenville shoot-out, Stokes won re-election in 1969 by a margin of over 3,700 votes over his Republican opponent Ralph J. Perk. However, Stokes' remaining tenure as mayor can be characterized as years of confrontation with city council. Racial polarization and rancor became the order of the day in council during the mayor's second term. Disillusioned black leaders withdrew from the Democratic Party and formed the 21st District Caucus. Louis Stokes, the mayor's brother had been elected to Congress in 1968, to represent Ohio's 21st Congressional District. White councilmen responded by forming a rival 22nd District Caucus, resulting in political deadlock. Supported by City Council President Anthony Garofoli, councilman Dennis Kucinich took a leadership roll in thwarting the mayor. As the legislative process deteriorated, new initiatives were doomed to failure. For example, Stokes was unable to obtain council approval for public housing or police reform and the public housing debate actually degenerated into a physical confrontation. Carl Stokes felt that his inability to reform the Cleveland Police Department represented his greatest failure as mayor:

> I took my election as a mandate to reform the Police Department. I saw as one of my most important tasks the reform of the police, the return to having the police as our protectors, men who would enforce the law, do their job, be responsive to the needs of the people. This great hope became my greatest frustration, my greatest failure.[19]

Additionally, fiscal problems began to plague the Stokes administration. Without business support for Cleveland: NOW!, anticipated federal funds did not materialize. Also, Cleveland was still feeling the effects of the Ohio Supreme Court decision in the *Park Investment Case* which denied assessing commercial and industrial real estate beyond the true cash value applied to residential property. Cleveland had for over a decade unconstitutionally assessed businesses more than homeowners. Based upon the logical belief that profits and the use of city services on a $100,000 commercial property would exceed that needed on a $100,000 residence, the city continued to tax corporations more than individuals in violation of state law until the court ruling. Cleveland lost millions of dollars in property tax revenues because of the Park Investment decision. Moreover, the bankruptcy of the Penn-Central Railroad reduced municipal and school revenues. Although the Cleveland schools are not under the control of the city government, any noticeable decline in a city's school system impacts housing values, credit ratings and overall the well-being of city residents and Penn-Central was the largest landholder in the city when she filed for bankruptcy protection.

Threatened by strikes by various Cleveland unions, the administration yielded to these demands despite inadequate revenues to cover these increased costs. Subsequent voter rejection of an additional half percent increase in the city income tax, perceived as Stokes' tax, while approving a 5.8 mill reduction in property taxes, set the stage for a California type Proposition 13 debacle. Voter rejection of Stokes' tax reform proposal and the acceptance of 5.8 mill tax expiration cost the city $200 million by 1979. These actions resulted in layoffs and charges of fiscal irresponsibility leveled at the mayor's office as Stokes' tenure came to an end.[20]

References

[1]Carl B. Stokes, *Promise of Power: A Political Autobiography* (New York, 1973) pp. 67—71, 226.

[2]John J. Grabowski and David D. Van Tassel, editors, *The Encyclopedia of Cleveland History* (Bloomington, Indiana 1987) p. 479, and *Plain Dealer*, April 3, 1994.

[3]See Appendix A for Bob Modic's "Officials of 44 Firms Decide Destiny of City," *Cleveland Press*, June 6, 1966. Consult Appendix B for Tom Andrzejewski's update "We're in the Black, but Streets are Lean and Mean," *Plain Dealer*, June 26, 1987. And note Appendix C for a list of the individuals and corporations that are members of Cleveland Tomorrow, "Investing in the Future Cleveland Tomorrow's Strategic Picture for the 90's," January, 1993.

Another useful source not included in the Appendixes are Tom Coscarelli's, Nancy M. Funk's, and Stephen Phillips' collaborative article "The Players Making the Moves," *Plain Dealer*, April 2, 1991.

[4]Stokes, pp. 1-13, 62-69. For a good assessment of Eaton's anti-establishment character, see George G. Condon's, *Cleveland, the Best Kept Secret* (Cleveland, 1981).

[5]Weinberg, pp. 72, 203.

[6]Zannes, p. 5.

[7]*Cleveland Press*, June 8, 1966. In November 1966, Locher was able to convince city council to approve a half percent city income tax that went into effect in January 1967.

[8]Weinberg, pp. 91, 191.

[9]*Cleveland Press*, June 7, 1966, and The Illuminating Company, a radical research group, including Roldo Bartimole, *The Cleveland Papers* (Cleveland, 1969) p. 15.

[10]See Appendix A, *Cleveland Press*, June 7 and June 8, 1966.

[11]*Illuminating*, pp. 13, 19. See also Roldo Bartimole, *Point of View*, June 26, 1963, p. 1.

[12]Jeffrey K. Hadden, Louis H. Masotti, and Victor Thiessen, "The Making of the Negro Mayors 1967," *Trans-Action Magazine* (St. Louis, 1968) and Weinberg, p. 78.

[13]Robert Allen, *Black Awakening in Capitalist America* quoted in *Illuminating*, p. 17.

[14]Weinberg, p. 114, *Illuminating*, p. 18, *Plain Dealer*, December 20, 1965, and *Cleveland Press*, June 6, 1966.

[15]Zannes, pp. 17, 34, 76. See also Appendix A.

[16]See *Business Week*, November 18, 1967, September 21, 1968, and December 19, 1970, *Time*, May 3, 1968 and February 28, 1969, *New Republic*, October 23, 1967, *Negro History Bulletin*, October, 1970, p. 148, *The Nation*, July 20, 1970, and Zannes, p. 34.

[17]*Illuminating*, p. 19.

[18]Stokes, pp. 224, 139 and 150.

Evans engineered the Glenville shoot-out to establish himself as "the" leader of black militants within Cleveland. Evans and his followers, the Black Nationalist Organization of New Libya, were sentenced to life terms. See Zannes, pp. xii-xiii, *Plain Dealer*, July 21, 1968, Gerald Kanner, editor, *1968 New Dictionary an Encyclopedic Summary of Contemporary History* (New York, 1969) p. 435, and Grabowski and Van Tassel, pp. 255-256.

[19]Stokes, p. 171.

[20]Zannes, pp. 227-228, and *Plain Dealer*, December 30, 1979.

THE STOKES LEGACY

Most Clevelanders tend to remember the fiscal problems and confrontation politics which exemplified the latter years of Stokes' tenure in office, but not his accomplishments as mayor, i.e. Cleveland: NOW! had generated federal funding for new construction, housing, and jobs. However, the element of singular importance to many, especially to white Clevelanders, was that Carl Stokes was a black mayor who left the city with a 27 million dollar debt. The racial polarization of the city seemed to come to the political forefront during the latter two years of the Stokes administration. With the establishment of the 21st District Caucus, even the mayor's attempt at raising the city's income tax became a racial issue. The legacy of Carl Stokes continued to linger negatively upon Cleveland politics, on October 1, 1975, the *Plain Dealer* reported that: "The Ghost of Carl B. Stokes lurks at the polls. Many Clevelanders, black and white, have predicted it may be awhile before there is another black mayor."[1]

Arnold Pinkney became irreconcilably linked to the Stokes legacy. During the Stokes' years, Arnold Pinkney had served as campaign manager for the mayor in 1967, and as executive assistant at City Hall. In the 1971 mayoral election, Pinkney, the black school board president, was the mayor's chosen successor. Pinkney employed the same strategy utilized by Carl Stokes in his unsuccessful 1965 campaign, essentially to avoid the Democratic primary, to run as an independent, maintain a black and liberal white coalition, and to benefit from the anticipated split in the white vote between the Democratic and Republican candidates.

However, in the Democratic primary, Carl Stokes endorsed James M. Carney, an industrialist and a past supporter of the mayor's campaigns. Stokes' decision to support Carney in the primary was principally determined on the grounds that he felt the other main contender for the Democratic nomination, Anthony Garofoli, was a racist. Anthony Garofoli was Stokes' antagonistic city council president and the endorsed Democratic candidate. The principal contributing factor to Garofoli's winning the support of the county Democrats was the absence of black representatives because of the establishment of the 21st District Caucus. In order to win support for Carney in the black areas of the city, Stokes drafted the following letter which was subsequently distributed by Carney workers:

> I am sure you are aware that I want Arnold
> Pinkney to succeed me as mayor in November. How-
> ever, Arnold is not in next Tuesday's Democratic party
> primary election, and we have the opportunity to
> remove from the final contest in November a man who
> would be extremely bad for Cleveland - Council
> President Anthony J. Garofoli, whose years in office
> have been devoted to racially dividing our city.
>
> As you know, part of the Ward Garofoli repre-
> sents is Murray Hill where we have had one disgusting
> and horrible racial incident after another.
>
> You can help make sure that Mr. Garofoli will
> not be around for the general election in November by
> casting your vote next Tuesday in the Democratic
> primary for a decent man, James M. Carney.
>
> Vote for James M. Carney in the Democratic
> primary on Tuesday, September 28, 1971.[2]

Thus, Stokes simultaneously sought to have Carney win the Democratic primary and Pinkney, another Democrat, the general election.

The subsequent Carney victory in the primary placed two
Democratic contenders in the general election, Carney and Pinkney as
an independent, against Ralph J. Perk who had won the Republican
primary. Utilizing an ethnic political base, Ralph Perk's strategy in the
general election was to advocate no new taxes, attack fiscal irresponsi-
bility, while fusing his opponents to Stokes - "Beat Carney, Pinkney,
Stokes. Vote for Perk." As a consequence of the Stokes primary endorsement, a large number of black voters supported Carney in the
general election, paving the way for a Perk victory. In November,
Perk received 38.7 percent of the votes cast, Pinkney 31.7, and Carney
28.7 percent.[3]

Carl Stokes' explanation for the Pinkney defeat was his inability to gain white support rather than solidify Cleveland's black vote:
"He had no white votes of his own to go with the big black vote I
muscled for him. He finished second in the November 1971 general
election, second to Ralph Perk, the man I had twice run ahead of."[4]
Similarly in the 1973 mayoral campaign, Ralph Perk attacked the
ghost of Carl Stokes. Once again maintaining his ethnic support, Perk
focused his campaign on fiscal responsibility and attacked his opponent James Carney for his association with Stokes.

Because of changes in Cleveland's election law, in the 1975
mayoral election, Arnold Pinkney could not run in a three-way race as
an independent as Stokes had in 1965. The adoption of Issue 1 in 1971,
which Ralph Perk sponsored, altered the law governing Cleveland's

mayoral elections. Issue 1 provided for a return to nonpartisan elections in the mayor's race, only the two leading candidates in the primary would be eligible for the general election.[5] Although ostensibly nonpartisan, Cleveland's elections (since the adoption of Issue 1) had a Democrat and a Republican finalist until the election of Michael White. Another example of the partisan nature of Cleveland's nonpartisan elections surfaced in 1973, when James Carney a finalists withdrew from the election. Rather than grant the third primary candidate a Socialist, an opportunity, the board of elections allowed the Democrats to nominate council clerk Mercedes Cotner to run against Perk. As the first female to make a bid to become mayor, Cotner had less than two weeks to prepare a campaign.

Many other political elements changed since Carl Stokes ran against Ralph Perk. In the 1969 election, Stokes was the incumbent, which enabled him to attract additional white support. For example: "Two lower-status white precincts in Cleveland which had given Stokes only minimal support in 1967 became pro-Stokes in 1969 after he had opened a much-desired playground in the area."[6] Stokes polled 22 percent of the white vote in 1969, up from 11 percent in 1965. In 1975, Arnold Pinkney challenged an incumbent. Perk received 8 percent of the black while Pinkney captured 12 percent of the white vote in 1975.[7]

What role did the Cleveland establishment play in the Pinkney election? According to Edward C. Banfield's and James Q. Wilson's analysis, the business community should not be overly influential in Cleveland politics:

> Thus at least three conditions are requisite to a high degree of business influence: (1) businessmen must have an interest in wielding local influence; (2) they must have a common set of goals, either because they agree or because they can be made to agree by some centralizing influence in the business community; and (3) they must control those resources valued by politicians and thus control the politicians. So little research has been done in large American cities that no general answer can be given to the question of how influential businessmen are. However, on the basis of what we know of such cities as Chicago, New York, Detroit, St. Louis, Cleveland and others, we feel safe in summarizing that it is the exception rather than the rule for all three conditions to exist in any large, diverse American city, particularly in the industrial North.[8]

Perhaps the incidents in Hough, the business community's disenchantment with Locher and their ability to manipulate Cleveland: NOW! finances met the Banfield and Wilson criteria in 1967.

In an interview with Arnold Pinkney, the school board president stated that he had an appointment with the establishment on the following day, October 15, 1975.[9] Prior to his endorsement interview with the *Plain Dealer*, Pinkney had supported the four-point program of Governor Rhodes which had been previously endorsed by the Greater Cleveland Growth Association and the *Plain Dealer*. The Rhodes proposals called for a massive capital spending program financed by a dramatic increase in the state's bonded indebtedness (Reagonomics 101). However, after the *Plain Dealer* endorsed Ralph Perk, Pinkney became sharply critical of the Governor's proposals. Further, Pinkney stated that if the Rhodes' issues were adopted, he would use the revenues for neighborhood improvement and increased services rather than Perk's focus on downtown projects, i.e. implementing the Halprin plan to renovate the downtown area. The latter program was supported by the Greater Cleveland Growth Association and its president Campbell W. Elliot, who advocated that such revenues should be utilized to stimulate the downtown area. For example, improvements to Public Hall and the Convention Center, Elliot insisted, were imperative to attract convention and trade shows.[10]

The issues during the 1975 campaign were similar to those in 1969: law and order and fiscal responsibility. Also, as in the 1969 general election, the racial issue was overtly suppressed by both Perk and Pinkney. In 1975, both candidates opposed school busing (not an issue in 1969), promised no new taxes, and advocated a need for greater police protection. In the latter issue of law and order, however, Pinkney sought to reform the police department by altering its bureaucratic structure to "weed out" corrupt and "insensitive" policemen, making the department more responsive to the citizenry.[11] Pinkney's approach to law and order was designed to appeal to both inner city residents as well as to middle class black and white neighborhoods.[12]

Of paramount importance in this election was an issue that both candidates agreed upon: their opposition to busing. Based on a survey of white registered voters conducted by this author, Pinkney lost the support of over 10 percent of the whites who voted for him for the school board in 1973 because they wanted to keep a school board president who opposed busing in charge of the Cleveland system. As one respondent explained her mayoral preference in 1975: "I don't really know at this point the way the city is going. At the time of the election, I voted for Perk to keep him out of the Senate and I also did not want to lose Pinkney from our school board. Since he is a fine member of the board, in fact, the best one on our board, and I knew his feelings were against busing." This comment indicates that busing was an extremely salient variable in the 1975 Cleveland mayoral election. Although many political observers in Cleveland felt that Ralph Perk's victory over Arnold Pinkney was attributed to Perk's ethnic heritage and to the racial polarization in the city, these remarks by a white Clevelander intimate that the issues raised during the campaign may have been more complex than a political race between a white incumbent verses a black school board president. According to this survey, Pinkney lost half his potential (Stokes, 1969) white support because these voters feared busing, and wanted to have a school board president and a mayor opposed to busing.[13]

On October 3, 1975, Stokes returned to Cleveland to speak before the City Club Forum, in fact his remarks made the front page headline of the *Plain Dealer*. At the City Club, Stokes lashed out against black leaders for failing to take the lead in directing Cleveland toward solving "human needs." Further, Stokes attacked Pinkney for helping Perk interject the "phony issue" of busing into the mayor's race. In addition, the former mayor assailed Cleveland's black leaders for diluting the black community's strength by selling out to the Democratic Party (the 21st District Caucus rejoined the regular Democrats in 1974). Yet the Stokes' legacy continued to be an issue in the election. It was reported that the co-chairman of the Cuyahoga County Democratic Party was "delighted with Stokes' remarks because the Democrats are starting a campaign to divorce Pinkney from Stokes to help Pinkney in the white community."[14]

During an interview, Arnold Pinkney emphasized that he differed from Stokes in many areas--political philosophy, community goals, and in individual political style. Unlike Stokes, Pinkney sought to win the mayor's office to promote economic gains rather than Stokes' attempts to use the office to "solve all problems." He also emphasized that Cleveland had changed since Stokes was mayor, particularly in the black community where the concern for economic goals outweighed social goals. Pinkney stressed his administrative skills as school board president and his business background as assets in the election. In these capacities, Pinkney perceived himself as a mediator and a negotiator, whereas Stokes was described as being "more political," thriving on the controversial.[15] The results of the 1975 election were best summarized by Phillip W. Porter in a *Parma Sun Post* article entitled "Race Still Issue in Perk Victory":

Arnold Pinkney ran as strong a campaign as anyone could against a man like Perk, who has the ethnic vote locked up, most of it coming from citizens who nominally call themselves Democrats. But the result was already decided when Perk came in a close second in the primary Sept. 30, when a half dozen minor candidates, including a couple of West Side Irishmen, were running. With the also-rans out, it became Perk vs. Pinkney, head to head. And the result was mostly racial. Let us not kid ourselves about it.

The city is still polarized, as Jim Carney said two years ago. And Perk was still running against Carl Stokes, though Stokes is long gone. Pinkney could not escape the fact that he was once Stokes' administrative assistant.[16]

Although there is ample evidence that the Cleveland business community helped to manipulate the 1967 election and to some extent, the Stokes administration itself, by opting out of Cleveland: NOW!, a number of other variables played an important part in determining Cleveland's mayoral elections. The Cleveland establishment was/is not a monolith. Despite the support of the Greater Cleveland Growth Association and the endorsement of the *Plain Dealer*, the Rhodes issues failed in the city and in Cuyahoga County. There were a number of other important issues that were also salient in the Stokes and Pinkney elections: the national media, race, ethnic voting behavior, Stokes' endorsement of Carney in 1971, the 21st District Caucus and the split in the Democratic Party, the Stokes legacy of confrontation politics, election changes, and the personal philosophies and goals of the two men.

References

[1]*Plain Dealer*, October 1, 1975.

[2]Zannes, p. 237.

[3]*Parma Sun Post*, November 13, 1975, *Plain Dealer*, October 1, 1975, and Zannes, pp. 243 and 250.

[4]Stokes, p. 247.

Perk also benefited in the 1971 mayoral election from the support of the firebrand councilman Dennis Kucinich. Kucinich founded an organization known as Democrats for Perk to strengthen Perks ethnic vote at the expense of Carney.

[5]*Plain Dealer*, October 1, 1975 and Eugene C. Lee, *The Politics of Non-partisanship, A Study of California City Elections* (Berkeley, 1960) p. 37.

Although Cleveland experienced a number of years of nonpartisan elections, in 1958 Cleveland's mayoral election became partisan and remained so until the adoption of Issue 1.

[6]Pettigrew, p. 109.

[7]*Plain Dealer*, November 5, 1975, and Pettigrew, pp. 99—100.

[8]Weinberg, p. 219.

[9]These statements were made during an interview that I conducted with Arnold Pinkney on October 14, 1975.

The *Plain Dealer* emerged as the largest newspaper in the city and the state in 1968. In 1982, the *Cleveland Press* ceased publication, leaving Cleveland with only one major newspaper. The *Press* was decidedly Democratic while the *Plain Dealer* especially on the national level tends to support Republican candidates.

[10]*Plain Dealer*, October 26, 1975.

[11]These statements were made when Arnold Pinkney spoke at Cuyahoga Community College - Western on October 14, 1975.

[12]Walter Williams, "The Crisis Ghetto," in Bryan T. Downes, editor, *Cities and Suburbs: Selected Readings in Local Politics and Public Policy* (Belmont, California, 1971), pp. 39-48.

[13]This random survey of over 330 white voting residents, corresponded closely to the actual vote recorded for Pinkney. In the sample 13.6 percent stated they voted for the school board president which compared favorably to exit polls which put this percentage at 12 percent. According to this telephone survey, 11.6 percent of these who voted for Pinkney for the school board in 1973, failed to support him for mayor in 1975. Almost 93 percent of this group supported neighborhood schools, to such an extent that this group was more

willing than either the pro-Pinkney or the anti-Pinkney sample to abandon state aid to maintain them. In 1978, the State of Ohio and the Cleveland Public School System was found guilty of deliberate acts of segregation and school busing was ordered to ameliorate the situation.

During the 1950's, school district's boundaries were deliberately re-drawn by the Cleveland School Board to force most white students to leave a racially mixed Rosedale Elementary School to attend nearby all-white schools. This author, a student at Rosedale, can personally attest to the changing racial composition which followed at the school.

[14]*Plain Dealer*, October 4, 1975.

[15]My interview with Pinkney..

[16]*Parma Sun Post*, November 13, 1975.

SOMEONE TAKE THE WHEEL

Ralph Perk became the first Republican elected to a county-wide office since 1934, when he was elected Cuyahoga County Auditor in 1962. Perk had previously defied Cleveland's conventional political logic when he served as a Republican city councilman from 1953 until his county-wide triumph. Ralph Perk deserves credit for revitalizing the Republican Party in Cuyahoga County. When Perk became the first Republican mayor in Cleveland since Harold Burton, he was able to transfer the auditors position to a picked successor, George Voinovich. Name recognition is an important asset for politicians, as an incumbent once stated: "I don't care what they say about me, as long as they spell my name right." In Cuyahoga County, no position has a greater opportunity to place a politicians name in front of the public eye than the auditor's office since every scale and gasoline pump in the county must have the auditor's inspection sticker in plain sight.

Using the safety of a four-year term and the awesome name recognition associated with the auditor's position, the Republicans began to chip away at the Democratic control of county offices during off-year elections. With limited resources, the Democrats were unable to defend all of their previous holdings. Once Voinovich was elected County Commissioner, the Republicans began playing musical chairs. When Voinovich joined the commissioner's office, Vince Campanella became auditor. Later when Voinovich resigned as commissioner to become Lieutenant Governor, Campanella took his commission seat, giving the auditor's office over to another Republican. Throughout this period, the county Democrats remained on the defensive. Many influential Ohio Republicans owe their political careers to Perk's ground-breaking victory in 1962.

Ralph Perk's tenure as mayor was characterized by a continuing deterioration of the fiscal integrity of the city, acquiescence to business interests, and political ineptitude. The financial problems plaguing the city had not been resolved and additional ones were just on the horizon. A steady loss of population, accelerated by un-taxable highway, educational, and county medical construction, continued to lower the tax base of Cleveland. A more immediate monetary problem for Perk was the destruction of the city-owned Municipal Light Plant's huge new generator which forced the city into purchasing electricity from the privately owned Cleveland Electric Illuminating Company. Adding to this cost was an expensive electrical tie-in between the two plants as the municipal indebtedness to local banks, particularly Cleveland Trust, skyrocketed.[1]

Unable to properly maintain services, valuable city assets would be given to others to control. Cleveland's management of the city's lake-front parks were given over to the State of Ohio and the municipal transit and sewer system were shifted to regional control. Similarly, the control over Cleveland-Hopkins International Airport was weakened by the creation of Greater Cleveland Regional Transit Authority (RTA). Every municipal asset literally from a to z seemed to be on the auction block, even Cleveland's aquarium and zoo became part of the Metroparks. Because of the city's budgeting problems, Perk did more to regionalize county government then all his predecessors. Although Cuyahoga County voted down a regional government by a narrow margin in 1969 and 1970, Perk became the champion of regionalization by offering municipal assets to the highest bidder.

City services were slashed and over four hundred policemen were eliminated to try to keep the city solvent. Regrettably, Mayor Perk had just instituted one of the most progressive police examinations in the nation when he introduced a testing process and psychological screening that resulted in police recruits mirroring the ethnic and racial composition of the city.[2] With the cutback in services and the steady monetary losses, the mayor was willing to rally behind any construction project that might indicate a municipal comeback. Most major construction efforts like the Justice Center, the expansion of the Metro-General Hospital and Cleveland State University, and a new downtown State office building were public not private endeavors.

Inflation, foreign competition, and rising energy costs began to adversely affect older manufacturing centers in the East and Mid-West (like Cleveland) more than the rest of the country. Shrinking profit margins in real dollars convinced many firms to cut production, labor costs, and capital investment. During the golden age of the conglomerates, some companies purchased diverse, unrelated, but hopefully profitable businesses to shield corporate executives from stockholder's wrath. These megalithic monstrosities felt little affinity for the distant communities where their nameplate appeared. Even though Perk was a Republican, most local businesses avoided making major investments in the city.

Desperate, the mayor accepted tax abatement as a means to promote corporate action. Ultimately, a major section of the downtown area was eliminated to construct the National City Bank building. However, with the city's acquiescence to tax abatement, no additional tax revenues were raised to support the Cleveland Public School System. Additionally, two of the structures removed, Bond's and the Roxy, had nostalgic value to many in the area. The Bond Clothing Company was probably Cleveland's premier commercial example of Art Moderne architecture, while the Roxy Theater appealed to some more prurient interests.

Ralph Perk did bring national attention to Cleveland. At a trade fair at the Cleveland Convention Center, the mayor's hair caught fire. This incident seemed to reinforce the negative images that Cleveland endured because firecrews had to be sent to a debris fire on the Cuyahoga River in 1969. In addition, Perk's wife refused to attend President Nixon's inaugural dinner because it was on the same night as her bowling banquet. Finally, his appointment to the Regional Sewer Board, Anthony Liberator, ended up on the FBI's ten most wanted list.

During his 1973 campaign, Perk made two promises to the people of Cleveland: not to run for higher office and not to raise taxes. His unsuccessful run for the United States Senate against John Glenn in 1974 and his request to increase taxes severely damaged his credibility with area voters. Perk's inability to raise revenues forced the mayor to increase Cleveland's municipal indebtedness to the state's legal limit by 1974, moreover, about $150 million of this debt was in short-term notes that were refinanced yearly.[3]

Unlike New York City which technically went into default in 1975, Cleveland had one important ally in Washington. President Richard Nixon's desire to keep a Republican mayor in charge of a major U.S. city resulted in the Forest City receiving millions of dollars of Federal revenue sharing funds. Perk took advantage of his party affiliation to make a credible pitch to host the 1976 Republican National Nominating Convention. Without adequate hotel space to house the delegates, he suggested leasing cruise ships to accommodate the conventioneers. With the fear of federally ordered busing clouding other issues, Perk won again in 1975, although one-half the registered voters stayed home.

Soon after the death of John Scalish, the undisputed head of organized crime in Cleveland, open warfare erupted between factions vying for control of the city's underworld. Since Scalish had not designated an heir, his top lieutenants chose a rather reluctant James Licavoli, as an interim leader. Licavoli (aka Jack White) was a former member of Detroit's Purple Gang and had long been associated with Cleveland's mob investments in Niles and Warren, Ohio. His main challenger was John Nardi, secretary-treasurer of the Vending Machine Service Employees Local 410, and a nephew of Anthony Milano (Consiglieri). Anticipating mob acquiescence, Nardi made a simultaneous move to become the head of the Teamsters Union at the expense of Jackie Pressor. But his willingness to ally with the flamboyant Irish numbers kingpin, Danny Greene, was to promote opposition and ultimately his undoing.

During the 1960's, Danny Greene had been forced from his leadership position in the International Longshoreman's Union because of substantiated charges of shakedowns, deliberate work stoppages, threats against stevedore company owners' children, and embezzlement. Danny Greene later joined Tony Liberatore in attempting to create a unified trash hauling enterprise, the Cleveland Solid Waste Guild but because of newspaper exposure, the mob was forced to abandon the project — at least temporarily. The publicity-seeking Greene eventually started his own business, Emerald Industrial Relations. When some unions stalled or caused trouble on a construction site, Greene would step in and guarantee labor peace for a price, many paid rather than suffer costly delays, including the Justice Center.

In 1975, the Northern Ohio Bank was another one of the victims of organized crime in Cleveland. The bank was forced to cease operation by authorities because of bad (unpaid mob) loans on its books and the bank president was imprisoned after pleading guilty to conspiracy and bank fraud charges.

Open warfare began after Nardi demanded a percentage of the gambling revenues generated by the Feast of the Assumption festivities held in Little Italy. Leo Morceri, a close friend and ally to Licavoli, objected to any deal with Nardi. This was the last time that Morceri was seen alive. Although his blood-soaked automobile was discovered soon thereafter, Morceri's body has never been located. A retaliatory blood bath ensued with both factions vying for control. The principle weapon of choice - the car bomb - was used to murder both Nardi and Greene (incidentally, Nardi's wife received $50,000 from the Ohio Crime Compensation Act). Ultimately, state and federal prosecutions reduced the criminal organization to a skeletal remnant of its former glory. Tony Liberatore was recently found guilty in Akron's U.S. District Court of engaging in labor racketeering and money laundering while leading Cleveland's organized crime family as a federal prisoner and he received a ten year sentence in March 1994. Although this confrontation ultimately resulted in decimating the top leadership of organized crime in the area during Perk's tenure, this conflict made Cleveland the bombing capital of the United States in 1976 and 1977.[4]

Most of Ralph Perk's much touted building projects, including a proposed jetport island in Lake Erie, never materialized. Residential construction ceased and demolition costs were running a million dollars a year. Further, as his third term ended, evidence of corruption surfaced within the Model Cities program and Perk's much publicized summertime crackdown on pornography and prostitution alienated some skeptical voters who questioned the mayor's motives. Finally, Ralph Perk's decision to sell the Municipal Power Plant to the Cleveland Electric Illuminating Company angered much of Cleveland's electorate.[5]

In the 1977 primary, Perk came in third, which eliminated him from contention in the general election. His two youthful challengers (either one of whom would become the youngest mayor of a major city) Dennis Kucinich and Edward Feighan, vied for the city's highest office. Clerk of Courts and former city councilman Kucinich narrowly won the mayor's race, defeating Edward Feighan a political unknown, by only three thousand votes.

To some Clevelanders Dennis Kucinich was a white knight, to others he was a court jester. But for all his good intentions and his faults, he understood who controlled the city. A true populist, Dennis Kucinich planned to confront the octopus by using the mayor's office as a club and if that failed, using his grass roots support to shame it into submission. Since the Stokes years and Cleveland: NOW!, there is a greater realization by area politicians as to the corporate involvement in city politics. As a councilman, Kucinich was one of those responsible for the confrontation politics that characterized the Stokes era after Glenville, and he was not a novice but a veteran of city politics with a keen understanding of the community power structure.

Other Cleveland politicians have built careers by knowing when to be a friend or foe to corporate interests. George Forbes, the man that held the position of City Council President longer than anyone in the city's history, including the Kucinich years, perhaps best represented this understanding. Forbes was undoubtedly the most powerful black politician in Cleveland during this period. He was like a willow knowing when to stand tall and when to bend to the wind. With Forbes you never questioned what he said, you looked at what was done as his confrontational rhetoric had little in common with political reality.

In the mayoral election, Dennis Kucinich, taking up the

populist banner, attacked tax abatement and redlining. During his tenure as mayor no tax abatement was granted; however, the only construction in the city was the expansion of the Orlando Bakery. His approach to redlining (the refusal of banks to grant loans to the city rather than suburban residents for renovation or new construction of new homes) was more direct, he publicly removed his own funds from one of the principal violators and encouraged every resident of Cleveland to follow his lead.

Table 7: Mortgages Per 100 Homes	
East Side	1.9
West Side	4.4
Total City	3.0
Inner Ring	4.8
Middle Ring	6.5
Outer Ring	9.6
Total Sububurbs	6.4
Total County	5.2

Source: *Plain Dealer*

In an attempt to disassociate himself with the past, he surrounded himself with a politically inexperienced staff, dubbed "Kiddy Hall" by the local media, their names still can kindle bad feelings for many corporate executives. Kucinich's chief political advisor, Bob Weissman, vindictively terminated a live broadcast by the city's most popular radio personality, Gary Dee. This kind of petty maneuvering seemed to dominate Kucinich's administration. However, his choice for Safety Director, Richard Hongisto, won him national recognition. Problems between the Cleveland Police Department and local, particularly minority, citizens were long standing in Hongisto the former sheriff of San Francisco with a proven reputation for understanding minorities, Kucinich seemed to have picked a winner.

Angered by the Kucinich administration's refusal to sell the Municipal Power Plant, the Cleveland Electric Illuminating Company demanded immediate payment of over twenty million dollars for electric services owed because of the previous shut-down of the city's generator. The only way the city could pay this debt was to have major banks rollover past debts (images of Cleveland: NOW! revisited), led by Cleveland Trust, the financial institutions refused; they had him and he knew it. When Kucinich refused to back down, Cleveland technically went into default. By refusing to submit to the Cleveland Trust's and Illuminating Company's blackmail, Cleveland became the first major city to default since the Great Depression. The corporate community felt a little national public relations problem was better than allowing Dennis to have his way.

There would be no silver-lining in the clouds that followed for Dennis Kucinich, as corporate Cleveland flexed its collective economic muscle. Sohio, one of the city's largest employers, canceled plans for a new corporate headquarters in the city and Republic Steel, another major employer, announced that it would build its proposed ore dock in Lorain, not Cleveland. Cleveland Trust's decision, at this time, to change her corporate title to AmeriTrust was not accidental.

With Murphy's Law prevailing, Richard Hongisto was fired because he apparently uncovered a deliberate attempt by the snow removal crews not to shovel in areas that did not vote for the mayor. With human lives at risk, Hongisto publicly exposed the inability of the city's safety forces to pursue life-threatening calls through snow-covered streets. Kucinich publicly admonished the chief and fired Hongisto This incident prompted a recall attempt to remove the mayor from office after his serving only one year. Although Kucinich successfully defeated the recall attempt by only 236 votes, his remaining year was uneventful.

Dennis Kucinich did have his moment of vindication when the people of Cleveland voted to retain control of the Municipal Light Plant rather than sell it to the Cleveland Electric Illuminating Company. In addition, the electorate approved a one half percent increase in the city's income tax. Cleveland's default, the lack of economic activity, political chicanery, and the recall election had taken their toll. Not surprisingly, Kucinich lost the 1979 mayoral race to the Republican challenger Lieutenant Governor George Voinovich.[6]

References

[1]See Appendix B for a poignant assessment of Cleveland's default.

Cleveland Electric Illuminating Company had sought to gain control of the Municipal Power System since the mid-1960's, *Cleveland Press*, June 9, 1966.

According to the findings of the Nuclear Regulatory Commission, the Illuminating Company violated federal anti-trust laws to gain control of the Municipal Light Plant. When this information was given to jurors in a later civil case brought by the city against CEI, all six jurists thought that the city deserved compensation. However, one juror resented the pressure placed on her by the others and voted for CEI to protest their actions.

[2]*Plain Dealer*, May 20, 1990, and July 29, 1994.

In 1977, Cleveland's non-white population represented 42 percent of the city's population but the percentage on the police department was only 9.3 percent. By comparison, Cincinnati's non-white population was 28 percent and on the police force 7 percent while St. Louis' more comparable 41 percent non-white residents were served by a police force that nearly doubled Cleveland's at 18 percent. Court ordered changes resulted in an increase in the number of non-whites on the Cleveland Police Force. By May 1990, Cleveland's Black police officers represented 23.5 percent of the department.

[3]*Plain Dealer*, December 30, 1979.

[4]See Appendix D for this author's assessment of the structure of organized crime in Cleveland during the mid-1970's.

[5]*Cleveland Press*, and the *Plain Dealer*, October 5, 1977.

Envisioning a futuristic Cleveland, Perk enthusiastically supported the jetport concept. But opposition soon emerged in Euclid which was slated to be decimated by a ten lane highway envisioned to become the islands major thoroughfare. Euclid is home to a large number of major manufacturing firms. Incidentally, Euclid has the largest Slovenian population in the world outside of Slovenia. In an effort to promote some momentum for the project, I telephoned Perk and offered the idea of a monorail as an alternative highway access. Perk allowed me to consult with members of RTA. Because of this meeting, Cleveland drafted a mass transit proposal that ultimately awarded a monorail to the city and mobile sidewalks to Cleveland-Hopkins. The monorail got lost in the transfer of power from Perk to Kucinich, the conflicts between Kucinich and city council and the city's default. When Cleveland refused the $60 million Federal project, it was awarded to Detroit. After a dozen years, Detroit connected her old downtown with the Renaissance Center with Cleveland's mono-rail.

⁶See Appendix B.

Organized labor overwhelmingly supported Dennis Kucinich. Cleveland's most politically active union, the United Automobile Workers (UAW), enthusiastically campaigned for the mayor's re-election.

In his future political endeavors, Kucinich remained labor's champion and local unions supported his political aspirations. Typical of this mutual understanding, Dennis Kucinich emerged as the most visible opponent to Mayor White's effort to privatize resurfacing and street repairs. *Plain Dealer*, May 17, 1994.

A CITY REBORN

George Voinovich lost in his first attempt to become Cleveland's mayor. In 1971, Voinovich ran against Ralph Perk in the Republican primary for mayor. When Perk was elected, he appointed Voinovich, a member the Ohio House since 1967, as his replacement for the auditor's position. After being elected to the auditor's office on his own credentials, Voinovich was elected county commissioner in 1976. Shortly thereafter, he became lieutenant governor in the states first tandem election. Prior to the 1977 election, the top two state offices were elected separately, so it was not uncommon to have a Republican governor and a Democratic lieutenant governor. After defeating Kucinich, Voinovich stepped down as lieutenant governor, leaving the top two positions in the state government vacant, with James Rhodes remaining as governor.

With Cleveland's default, Voinovich was able to clear the decks of the fiscal improprieties that had characterized the city's finances for years. Desperate mayors had for years cannibalized capital improvement bond funds for general expenses.[1] Cleveland executives willingly loaned Voinovich their services to study and recommend improvements for the administration of city government. By heeding their advice and suggestions, Voinovich forged an alliance that transformed the city.

Eight local banks granted the city a bridge loan by purchasing 14 year notes to enable the new administration enough time to restore financial integrity to the city. When a complete audit of the books revealed a $110 million deficit, Voinovich reorganized city departments, and instituted new accounting procedures which included internal auditing. In 1981, Cleveland voters approved an increase in the city's income tax to two percent. Financially, Cleveland's house was in order. Finally, on June 25, 1987, Mayor George Voinovich, in a public ceremony, burned copies of default documents, marking the end of state control over the city's borrowing and spending.

Although Cleveland's electorate had voted to keep the Municipal Light Plant (Gary Dee's "Puny Muny"), Voinovich continued to negotiate the facilities' sale to the Cleveland Electric Illuminating Company (CEI). When Voinovich refused the company's offer, the Illuminating Company retaliated and abandoned its pledge to relocate its corporate headquarters in downtown Cleveland (Tower City) and threatened to move its executive offices out of the city to a suburban location but Voinovich held firm and pursued the city's lawsuit against the company.

Unlike 1977, corporate Cleveland supported the mayor. High electric rates had burdened local firms for years and the escalating costs of CEI's Davis-Besse and Perry Nuclear Plants promised even higher increases in the future. Further, the Illuminating Company's chief supporter, AmeriTrust, was in no position financially (a few bad Colorado investments) to push the administration. When it was done, CEI changed its name to the Illuminating Company and stayed in its old corporate headquarters. Voinovich changed the name of "Puny Muny" to Cleveland Public Power and enlarged and expanded its operations into the eastern portions of the city.

During the 1980's some fundamental changes took place in the city's electoral processes. Cleveland voters reduced the size of City Council from 33 to 21 members and more importantly, the citizens lengthened the terms of the council and the mayor to four years. For years Cleveland mayors were limited by a two-year term. Within a year of being inaugurated, a mayor would need to prepare re-election plans as problems tended to be ignored as election prospects and promises filled the political arena. Beginning in 1981, the city's executive and legislative terms were extended to four years.

Kucinich's defeat may have been a relief to the business community but it also was an awakening as two decades of relative inertia were followed by remarkable growth. During the 80's, Cleveland witnessed its greatest period of growth since the 1920's. Sohio built her new corporate headquarters, the BP America building, renamed after British Petroleum acquired Sohio, is actually the largest structure, in total area in the city. Richard and David Jacobs built the Galleria, a new enclosed downtown shopping mall attached to Erieview, and the Cesar Pelli designed Society Center, the 57-story structure surpassed the Terminal Tower as the tallest building in Cleveland. Later the Jacobs brothers outbid the grandson of Cyrus Eaton to purchase the Cleveland Indians and planned an even larger structure, the AmeriTrust Building. When Society bought out AmeriTrust and the economy slumped, these plans were delayed, until a new federal courthouse or the originally designed 60-story _____ office tower or casino was completed in 1996 for the city's bicentennial celebration. Albert Ratner's Tower City which included a RTA-linked station, Ritz Carlton Hotel, and a huge shopping complex, completed the third element of the Van Sweringens plan for Terminal Tower. Eaton Square and North Point, the former site of the *Cleveland Press* building, which became the new headquarters for the second largest law firm in the nation (Jones, Day, Reavis & Pogue), all attest to the revitalization of downtown Cleveland.

During the 1970's and 1980's, the city's efforts to restore Playhouse Square as a performing-arts center became the nation's largest undertaking of its kind. Funding for this huge project came from grants from the National Endowment for the Arts, the Cuyahoga County commissioner's, private and corporate donations, and from local foundations. The County bought the Loew's Building and the Cleveland Foundation purchased the Bulkley Building in 1982.[2] The recovery of the theater complex, mirrored the city's revival.

This redevelopment was not limited to the downtown area. The massive expansion of the Cleveland Clinic, the largest privately owned hospital in the nation, and the building of the new Cleveland Play House opened a corridor of new construction (some heavy-handed stuff here) to Severance Hall. In the 1960's the owners of a restaurant chain known as the Spaghetti Factory, approached Cleveland Trust for a loan to open a similar establishment here. Despite the restaurants success in Toronto and San Francisco, the bank refused the request based upon the mistaken belief that no one would venture to Cleveland for an evenings entertainment. For years Pickle Bills fought a losing battle with banks and the city administration to open up the Flats to development. In the 80's, the Cleveland Flats, the near west side near the Cuyahoga River came alive. Today looking across the Cuyahoga River from Jeff Jacobs' Powerhouse, Shooters, or the Nautica complex, it would be nearly impossible to believe that someone could have questioned the vitality of the Flats and the nearby Warehouse District which abounds with activities like the Hilarities Comedy Club, lofts and refurbished office buildings.

Projects actually left the drawing board; the Inner Harbor was built, and the first portion of the Great Lakes Museum became a reality. In addition, the much delayed construction of the I.M. Pei's designed Rock and Roll Hall of Fame and Museum began in 1994. The Museum is scheduled for completion in September 1995.

National recognition followed Cleveland's accomplishment as the city was thrice awarded the distinction of being nationally acclaimed as the All-American City in 1982, 1984 and again in 1986 under Voinovich. Further, the mayor was elected to lead the National League of Mayors and City Managers and U.S. News and World Report raised the possibility of George Voinovich serving as George Bush's vice presidential running mate in 1988 to appeal to ethnic and urban voters.

Civic pride was also evident when this area outvoted other cities by a margin of twenty to one in a national newspaper poll to secure Cleveland as the location for the Rock and Roll Hall of Fame and Museum. The importance of having such an attraction probably has not yet permeated to the general public but Ohio is the third most visited state in the nation, behind California and Florida. Moreover,

Cleveland is the thirteenth most visited city in the United States attracting more visitors than New Orleans, Virginia Beach, or Las Vegas.[3]

This renewed pride in the city has also benefited from national media attention and from successful sports teams. A Cinderella season for Cleveland State University's basketball team enabled the Vikings to win national prominence when they were represented as one of the "Sweet Sixteen" during the "March Madness" of college basketball tournament play in 1986. The summer of 1986 also witnessed the resurgence of the Cleveland Indians and the year ended with the Cleveland Browns, twelve and four, the best record in the American Football Conference. In January 1987, *Time* called the Cleveland Browns the "Success Story of the Year." After a double overtime victory over the New York Jets, the Cleveland Browns advanced to the AFC playoff game against the Denver Broncos, though the Broncos defeated the Browns in overtime, the city's support for the team bordered on a frenzy, a unity unparalleled in this city since the 1950's.

The Cleveland Force won its division in the Indoor Soccer League, although it was eliminated in the playoffs. In the Spring of 1987, *USA Today* optimistically predicted that the Cleveland Indians would win the Eastern Division. Sadly for fans, the closest that the Cleveland Indians came to a World Series, between 1987 and the Spring of 1994, flowed from the pen and celluloid of David S. Ward. Ward, a Clevelander, wrote and directed "Major League." The sequel "Major League II" had its world premier at the Palace Theater on Playhouse Square in late March 1994.

The kingdom of the two Georges, Council President George Forbes and Mayor George Voinovich, continued to grow but not unabated. Urban Development Action Grants (UDAG) and tax abatement spurred on an unparalleled building expansion within the city. President Jimmy Carter increased federal revenue sharing aid to older cities like Cleveland but under President Ronald Reagan state and urban assistance dollars were dramatically slashed. However to provide a temporary cushion for the loss of Federal revenue sharing money, the Reagan administration provided UDAG funding for specific projects and the Voinovich administration took full advantage of this program, snaring the lions share of UDAG grants. In the final year that the Federal program was in operation Cleveland received $38 million of UDAG's national total of $50 million.

Both Georges worked to complete the missing link in downtown development, the Midtown Corridor. By fusing downtown construction to the state-of-the-art Cleveland Play House, Cleveland Clinic and University Circle, the Midtown Corridor seemed finally to unify the major eastern and downtown cultural areas of the city. This type of development contributed to Cleveland being labeled by Prentice Hall Travel Books as the twelfth most livable city in the nation and recognized as the twelfth hottest home real estate market in the country.[4] For the regal duo, their cooperative efforts resulted in accomplishments designed to promote their respective political careers, Voinovich for Governor and Forbes for mayor.

Additionally, George Forbes was nearly single-handedly responsible for the successful negotiations between suburban mayors and the State of Ohio in promoting the return of Figgie International, a *Fortune 500* company, to relocate on city-owned land in what became known as Chagrin Highlands during the waning days of the Voinovich administration. Although Forbes could count on business support for his mayoral bid, many Clevelanders felt that a number of important issues had been ignored during the duel monarchy. To divert attention from growing public complaints about slow police response time and charges that the police allowed drugs to be sold to East side neighborhoods,[5] the City Council President supported the allocation of nine millimeter weapons to policemen. Although this action won police support for the Forbes mayoral bid, it did little to allay citizen concerns.

Although a few upwardly mobile suburbanites began moving back to the city's rehabilitated Ohio City, warehouse lofts, and condominiums in the Flats, most Cleveland neighborhoods were ignored. Development dollars flowed into downtown projects while residential areas were neglected by the Voinovich administration. Furthermore, redlining by Cleveland banks continued to such an extent that the city ranked third in discriminating against blacks of all major urban areas. Only 15 percent of the home loans made in Cuyahoga County by AmeriTrust were awarded to properties in Cleveland.[6]

Table 8: Black to White Loan Rejections

	Black Rejection Rate	White Rejection Rate	Black-White Rejection Rate
1. Milwaukee	24.2%	6.2%	3.90:1
2. Pittsburgh	31.2%	8.2%	3.80:1
3. Cleveland	31.4%	8.4%	3.74:1
4. Chicago	27.6%	7.6%	3.63:1
5. Detroit	32.5%	9.1%	3.57:1
U.S. Average	23.7%	11.1%	2.14:1

Source: *U.S. News & World Report*, February 27, 1989

In the 1989 mayoral campaign, the Council President was challenged by a relatively obscure councilman, Michael White. White surprised many political analysts by his strong primary showing over a number of veteran politicians. George Forbes' close association with downtown development and corporate Cleveland netted him a campaign war chest more than doubling that of his opponent, but Michael White counter punched by promoting neighborhood development, attacking bank redlining and corporate abatement policies that reduced Cleveland Public School revenues and by challenging the slow response time of the Cleveland Police Department. In the final tally, Michael White recorded the victory, winning by over 17,000 votes.

As mayor, Michael White moved dramatically. Although tax abatement was granted for the proposed AmeriTrust Center, this tax deferment was linked to guaranteed residential loans for Cleveland neighborhoods. Although he attempted to increase law enforcement response time by hiring new recruits and by transferring specialized units to basic patrol, early retirements and fiscal problems resulted in an overall decline in the number of police personnel. To combat the spread of drugs and gangs over 500 suspected drug houses were boarded up in the city neighborhoods during Michael White's first term in office.

Further the Cleveland mayor won suburban support for increasing the county-wide sin tax on liquor and cigarettes to finance the Gateway Project. Gateway entailed building a new stadium and arena for the Cleveland Indians and the Cleveland Cavaliers. Prior to completing Gateway, the Cleveland Indians played in the largest and argumentatively the most fan unfriendly baseball facility in the major leagues, the Cleveland Municipal Stadium, while the Cavaliers performed at the Richfield Colosseum in Summit County. In addition, White promoted Cleveland as the site for the 1992 Democratic Convention.

Although the overall US economy stalled in the early 1990's, White was able to work effectively with the business community. Negotiating a compromise with the developers of AmeriTrust's tax abatement won the mayor high marks. Subsequent negotiations with the owners of the Cleveland Cavaliers and the Cleveland Indians, and the County Commissioners were also fruitful when problems arose during the construction of Gateway. When White nominated Bob Weissman to his cabinet perhaps more than a few eyebrows were raised, but there seemed to be a realization that it was not 1979.

Based upon a proposal sent by this author, the mayor and the county commissioners established a Sports Commission to promote Cleveland as a prime location for sporting events. By combining the areas College and University sports facilities with Gateway and the Municipal Stadium, the county has the training grounds and playing fields to serve as host to events as large as the, Pan American and Good Will Games. Established in 1992, this sports panel was instrumental in re-securing Cleveland's roll as the host for the Cleveland Grand Prix, a world class Indy-car race held in the city since 1982.

A similar suggestion by this author to create a Gambling Commission to regulate and license casino operations in the county prior to a state-wide vote has been deemed inappropriate by the Cuyahoga County Commissioner's legal department until the General Assembly grants such authority to local officials. During the past five years casino gambling has been legalized in numerous locations including: Windsor, Canada, Indiana, Illinois, Iowa, Mississippi, Missouri, and New Orleans. Unlike Alan Spitzer's ill fated statewide gambling referendum which was supported by only Cuyahoga, Lake and Lorain counties in 1990, a majority of Ohioans will vote to legalize gambling statewide, according to University of Cincinnati polling.[7] Therefore a preliminary study oriented gaming commission seemed/seems appropriate to determined the parameters that would govern the location, number, scope, disposition of revenues prior to an entrepreneur free-for-all.

Overall, the city's economy remains sound. The metropolitan area ranks fourth in the nation in the number of *Fortune 500* companies headquartered in greater Cleveland, and the state ranks third in manufacturing despite a fifty percent cutback in manufacturing jobs over the last three decades. Ohio led all states and the Cleveland CMSA ranked third among the top ten metropolitan areas in expanding or attracting new plants in 1993.[8]

Cleveland's economic and political health improved under George Voinovich, but socially, the former mayor's record was abysmal. According to the U.S. Labor Department, Cleveland generally and blacks specifically were not beneficiaries of the city's building boom in the 80's. In 1990, 13.8 percent of the city's residents were unemployed, with 9 percent of her white and 20.7 percent of her black workers unemployed, which corresponded to the Equal Employment Opportunity Commission's report that nationwide blacks were the chief victims of corporate layoffs during the 1990-91 recession.[9]

Mayor White aggressively tried to deal with the city's social concerns, persuading developers to construct over 2000 new homes the most residential construction seen in Cleveland since the end of the Korean War. The building of a new East Side Market and Church Square selectively revitalized east side neighborhoods, while granting tax abatement to a developer to build the Wyndham Playhouse

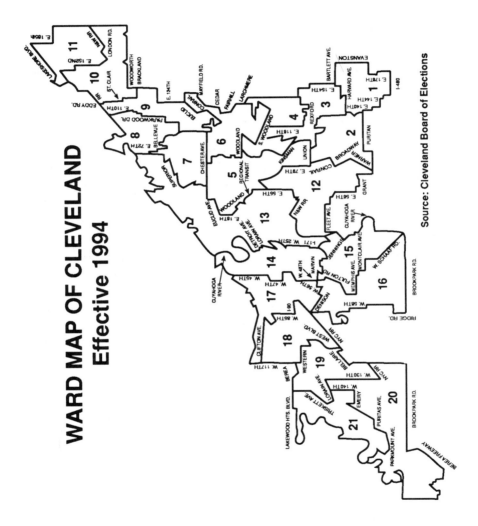

WARD MAP OF CLEVELAND
Effective 1994

Source: Cleveland Board of Elections

Square Hotel kept downtown projects on track. In addition, Michael White's relentless effort to convince banks to end redlining of selective Cleveland neighborhoods resulted in residential loan commitments by financial institutions to city residents exceeding one billion dollars by January 1994.[10]

White's efforts were recognized nationally. By 1991, Cleveland, "the Comeback City" was suggested as a potential vacation destination for Las Vegas residents and in 1993, she was once again chosen as an All-American City. Cleveland was actually the first recipient of the All-American award when the program was first introduced in 1949. Michael White's successful homebuilding efforts won the city the Ford Foundation's highest award for innovations in state and local government in 1993. By 1994, tourist income more than doubled for Cuyahoga County. In 1986 tourism generated only $1.6 million for the county, whereas $3.7 million was raised in 1993.[11]

Cleveland has often served as an inspiration to others in the quest for equality between the sexes. On the lighter side, Cleveland's 9 to 5 was a major contributor to the script of the 1980 smash comedy "Nine to Five"and it's spinoff television sitcom. More importantly in October 1993, the Gateway complex was commended by the Labor Department's Women's Bureau representative Karen Nussbaum, for becoming the nation's first project to fulfill the fifteen year federal goal of having 6.9 percent female participation on a construction site.[12]

In November 1993, the mayor won an unprecedented election sweep. White defeated his mismatched opponent David Lee Rock in a walk and every potential City Council challenger lost to an incumbent. For the first time in the 157 year history of the city's legislative assembly every council representative was re-elected and in their opening session the City Council re-elected Jay Westbrook as their president. Moreover, all four mayoral endorsed school board members on the Vision 21 slate and were victorious completing a electoral sweep for the mayor.[13]

The mayor established a good working relationship with council during his first term. White began his second by strong-arming the City Council into adopting a .4 mill tax hike on city residents to increase the number of police officers by 150, by announcing his intentions through a press release rather than consulting council he angered many in the representative assembly. Although few voted against the politically popular proposal, the City Council managed to re-establish a measure of balance at City Hall; Councilwoman Fannie M. Lewis probably said it best: "I don't have to be like the 'Free Stamp' (sculpture) for the other side of the hall over here."[14]

Mayor White seemed to get the message, but his commitment to police reform sent a similar message to the Cleveland Police Department.

Since improving police response time mandated increasing the departments presence in residential areas, non-essential police personnel in clerical and low level managerial positions were replaced by civilians. The Cleveland Police Patrolman's Association resisted both chief Kovacic's and the mayor's reform efforts through delays and threatened early retirement (accumulated sick and vacation days can double a policeman's final salary). Early in his second term, Michael White asked for and received the resignation of police chief Edward Kovacic.

After a national search, the mayor chose Cleveland's first black police chief, Patrick Oliver who had previously served as a highway patrolman until he was chosen as chief of the 70-officer Metroparks rangers in 1989, to head the Cleveland Police Department in March. By May 1994, Oliver selected his top aides, which included appointing the first women deputy chief, Kathryn T. Mengel, and announced his intension to make Cleveland the first major city to seek national police accreditation. Indicative of the difficulties involved in reforming the department, police unions immediately denounced two of the chief's choices as outsiders (Cleveland Heights and East Cleveland) and criticized the reduction in rank of veteran officers.[15]

Moreover, Michael White aggressively worked to improve the Cleveland Public School System, actively campaigning for a reform slate that succeeded in ending some forced busing within the city for the 1993-1994 school year. Further, the mayor successfully encouraged corporate involvement in the system. No recent Cleveland mayor has risked as much political capital as White has to reform an agency that he has no direct control over. However, a city's school system affects housing patterns and neighborhoods far more than any office tower.

By March, the mayoral backed Vision 21 board submitted a proposal to reform the school district and end forced busing for Cleveland school children that was accepted by Cleveland's Federal District Court. The new board and Superintendent Sammie Cambell Parrish sought to capitalize upon the momentum generated by the election and federal court decision by placing a 12.9 mill levy on the May 1994, primary ballot. Skeptical voters, accustomed to decades of political rhetoric, inertia and ineptitude by previous boards and administrations were swayed by an organized opposition to the tax hike which seemed to captivate the attention of the local news media to reject the proposal. Although Michael White actively campaigned for the levy and the citizens of Cleveland realized the importance of improving the public school system, in a political campaign it often requires as many as six positive statements to overcome a single negative comment. Therefore, the air-time granted to opposition late in campaign benefited the nay-sayers. For most Clevelanders the mayor's commitment to educational reform seemed right on the mark.

By opening day at Jacobs Field, Mayor White's Gateway project began to permanently and positively affect the city's economy. Before President Clinton threw out the first pitch on opening day, nearly two million tickets representing almost 56 percent of the seasons seating capacity had been purchased by eager fans. The Regional Transit Authority completed an enclosed walkway from the rapid transit linked Tower City to Gateway which was used by nearly half of the spectators and nine new restaurants employing some 450 workers had opened for sports patrons by April 1994. With the fall opening of the accompanying downtown Gateway home of the Cleveland Cavaliers these endeavors will not become seasonal aberrations. For you trivia buffs, Bill Clinton was the first American President ever to witness a Cleveland Indians game, incidentally the Indians won 5 to 4 in eleven innings defeating the Seattle Mariners before a capacity crowd.

Michael White won the support of city residents by his determination to improve the lives of ordinary citizens by focusing his attention upon the social problems long ignored by previous mayors; and his first term successes bordered on the legendary. But after his second term landslide victory, White's heavy-handed tactics with city council and city workers have increasingly raised questions about his leadership style. Hopefully the mayor will retain his commitment, despite the cost, to improve the city's educational system and reform the police department - the issues that originally captivated the admiration of the Cleveland electorate.

Unlike past visionary mayors like Celebrezze, Burke and Perk, labor oriented chief executives like Locher and Kucinich, and business oriented mayors like Stokes and Voinovich, White has attempted to find a middle ground, where neighborhood development spurred on by bank loans, churches, block grants and private developers, a responsive police and educational system paralleled downtown development. Undoubtedly a surprise to many, with the final pieces of the modern Cleveland bicentennial puzzle fitted into place what emerges is the suburbanization of the city with individual neighborhoods benefiting from a re-emergent downtown for the 200th birthday of Moses Cleaveland's vision.

References

[1]*Plain Dealer*, December 30, 1979.

[2]Ned Whelan, *Cleveland Shaping the Vision* (Chatsworth, California, 1989), *Downtown Magazine*, November, 1989, and Grabowski and Van Tassel pp. 771-2.

[3]*U.S. Air Magazine*, January, 1990.

[4]*Plain Dealer*, October 26, 1989, and *U.S. News and World Report*, April 9, 1990.

[5]*Cleveland Magazine*, July, 1989.

[6]*Newsweek*, September 9, 1991.

[7]According to a poll conducted by the University of Cincinnati, 54 percent of Ohioans will vote to support casino gambling statewide. *Plain Dealer*, December 14, 1993. The proposal to establish a gambling commission was sent to Mayor White and the County Commissioners, in February 1994.

[8]*Plain Dealer*, February 1, 1992, and October 7, 1993. According to *Site Selection and Industrial Development* (February, 1994) Ohio created 689 new plants or expansions while the Cleveland CMSA created 107, *Plain Dealer*, February 5, 1994. According to the Greater Cleveland Growth Association the 36 largest employers in Greater Cleveland are:

Federal Government	18,500	Dillard's (Higbee's)	4,530
Ford Motor Co.	10,896	Kaufmann's	
Catholic Diocese of Cleveland	10,000	(May Co. of Cleveland)	4,500
The Cleveland Clinic Foundation	9,900	Summa Health System	4,439
Cleveland Board of Education	9,673	Case Western Reserve	
Cuyahoga County Government	9,232	University	4,253
The MetroHealth System	8,328	Fred W. Albrecht Grocery Co.	4,000
City of Cleveland	8,226	Nestle Enterprises, Inc.	3,407
University Hospitals Health		Akron Board of Education	3,400
Systems, Inc.	7,640	United Parcel Service	
State of Ohio	7,630	of America, Inc.	3,314
LTV Steel Co.	7,500	National City Bank	3,300
Riser Foods, Inc.	6,500	Babcock & Wilcox	3,100
First National Supermarkets	6,451	American Greetings Corp.	3,050
Society Corp, Key Corp.	6,275	Blue Cross & Blue Shield	
Centerior Energy Corp.	6,200	of Ohio	3,000
The Goodyear Tire & Rubber Co.	5,937	Brown Derby, Inc.	3,000
Ohio Bell Telephone Co.	5,309	Progressive Corp.	3,000
Meridia Health System	5,000	GE Lighting	2,975
University of Akron	4,677	Greater Cleveland Regional	
General Motors	4,550	Transit Authority	2,900

Source: *Cleveland Magazine, 1994 City Guide*

[9]*Plain Dealer*, May 16, 1991, and September 16, 1993.

[10]*Plain Dealer*, January 20, 1994.

[11]*Las Vegas Review-Journal/Sun,* August 25, 1991, *Plain Dealer,* February 4, 1994 and Ford Foundation, 1993 *Inovations in State and Local Government* (New York, October, 1993).

Naming rights for the Gateway stadium and arena were purchased for $10 million each by Richard Jacobs and the Key Corporation-Society National, *Parma Sun Post,* March 24, 1994.

[12]*Plain Dealer,* October 9, 1993.

[13]*Plain Dealer,* November 3, 1993 and January 4, 1994.

Many elements from a slow response to snow removal to a contending major league sports team affect political outcomes in Cleveland. On election day in November 1993, the Cleveland Browns were 5 and 2 and appeared to be play off bound. Unbeknownst to most Clevelanders, the Cleveland Crunch, the city's professional soccer team came within one game of winning the NPSL Championship in April, with an assist from John Donoghue, "Pay Attention to the Crunch," *Plain Dealer,* October 20, 1993.

On April 27, 1994, the Crunch defeated the St. Louis Ambush to win the NPSL championship, setting off pandemonium in the Cleveland State University Convocation Center for the 11,162 fans in attendance. The Crunch brought the city her first national championship in 30 years; Cleveland had not secured a league crown in any sport since the Browns won the NFL title in 1964, *Plain Dealer,* April 28, 1994.

For a list of the 1994—1998 Cleveland City Council members, see Appendix E.

[14]*Plain Dealer,* December 7, 1993 and January 4, 1994.

After a three month hiatus, Michael White again clashed with city council over campaign finance reform. When the legislative body refused to certify charter amendment petitions, the mayor initiated legal proceedings against council. Voting irregularities forced the city's chief executive to quickly abandon litigation and seek a negotiated settlement. However, the mayor's actions weakened his rapport with council and strained his relationship with Council President Jay Westbrook who had consistently sought compromise over confrontation. See Brent Larkin's "Echoes in Council Chamber White's Words Boomerang," *Plain Dealer,* March 6, 1994.

[15]*Plain Dealer,* May 18-19, 1994.

**Your comments, corrections or criticism are welcome. Please direct your suggestions or inquiries to the author at Cuyahoga Community College's Western Campus.

CUYAHOGA COUNTY
1990

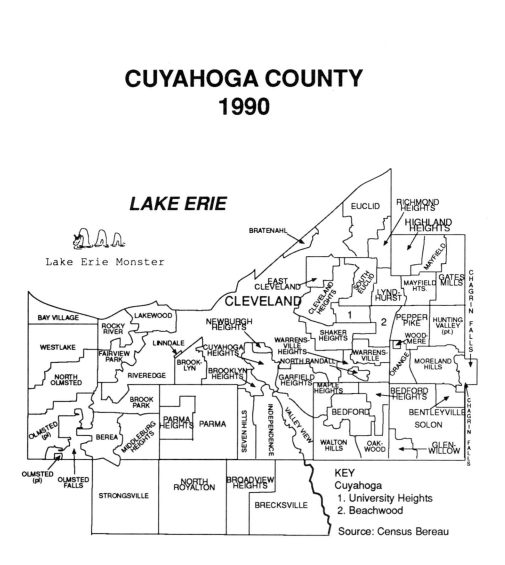

LAKE ERIE

Lake Erie Monster

BAY VILLAGE

LAKEWOOD

ROCKY RIVER

BRATENAHL

EUCLID

RICHMOND HEIGHTS

HIGHLAND HEIGHTS

MAYFIELD

GATES MILLS

MAYFIELD HTS.

EAST CLEVELAND

CLEVELAND

CLEVELAND HEIGHTS

SOUTH EUCLID

LYND-HURST

WESTLAKE

FAIRVIEW PARK

LINNDALE

NEWBURGH HEIGHTS

CUYAHOGA HEIGHTS

BROOK-LYN

1

2

PEPPER PIKE

HUNTING VALLEY (pt.)

WOOD-MERE

NORTH OLMSTED

RIVEREDGE

BROOKLYN HEIGHTS

SHAKER HEIGHTS

WARRENS-VILLE HEIGHTS

WARRENS-VILLE

ORANGE

MORELAND HILLS

NORTH RANDALL

GARFIELD HEIGHTS

MAPLE HEIGHTS

BEDFORD HEIGHTS

BROOK PARK

PARMA HEIGHTS

PARMA

SEVEN HILLS

INDEPENDENCE

VALLEY VIEW

BEDFORD

BENTLEYVILLE

SOLON

OLMSTED (tw)

OLMSTED (pl)

OLMSTED FALLS

BEREA

MIDDLEBURG HEIGHTS

WALTON HILLS

OAK-WOOD

GLEN-WILLOW

CHAGRIN FALLS

CHAGRIN FALLS

STRONGSVILLE

NORTH ROYALTON

BROADVIEW HEIGHTS

BRECKSVILLE

KEY
Cuyahoga
1. University Heights
2. Beachwood

Source: Census Bereau

108

PART III

CLEVELAND

Standard Metropolitan Statistical
Area/Primary Metropolitan
Statistical Area

CLEVELAND: SMSA/PMSA
1990

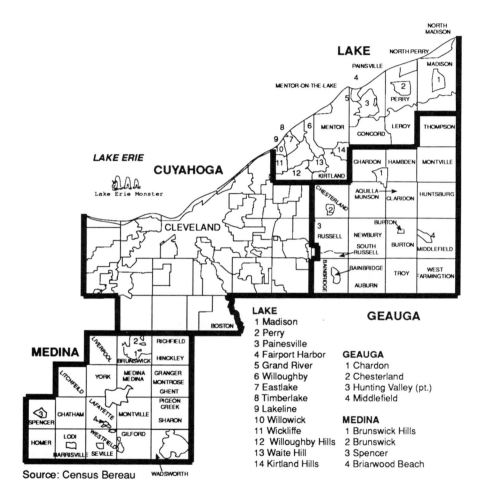

NORTH
MADISON

LAKE   NORTH PERRY

PAINSVILLE   MADISON

4   2   1

MENTOR-ON-THE-LAKE   PERRY

5   3

8   6   MENTOR   LEROY   THOMPSON

9   7   CONCORD

10   14

LAKE ERIE   11   13   CHARDON   HAMBDEN   MONTVILLE

CUYAHOGA   12   KIRTLAND   1

Lake Erie Monster   CHESTERLAND   AQUILLA   HUNTSBURG

MUNSON   CLARIDON

2   BURTON

CLEVELAND   3   RUSSELL   NEWBURY   4

SOUTH   BURTON   MIDDLEFIELD

RUSSELL

BAINBRIDGE   BAINBRIDGE   TROY   WEST

AUBURN   FARMINGTION

BOSTON

LIVERPOOL   2   RICHFIELD   **LAKE**   **GEAUGA**

1   1 Madison

MEDINA   BRUNSWICK   HINCKLEY   2 Perry

3 Painesville

LITCHFIELD   YORK   MEDINA   GRANGER   4 Fairport Harbor   **GEAUGA**

MEDINA   MONTROSE   5 Grand River   1 Chardon

GHENT   6 Willoughby   2 Chesterland

PIGEON   7 Eastlake   3 Hunting Valley (pt.)

LAFAYETTE   CREEK   8 Timberlake   4 Middlefield

3   CHATHAM   MONTVILLE   SHARON   9 Lakeline

SPENCER   10 Willowick   **MEDINA**

LODI   WESTFIELD   GILFORD   11 Wickliffe   1 Brunswick Hills

HOMER   12 Willoughby Hills   2 Brunswick

HARRISVILLE   SEVILLE   13 Waite Hill   3 Spencer

14 Kirtland Hills   4 Briarwood Beach

Source: Census Bereau   WADSWORTH

110

POPULATION, DEMOGRAPHIC, ETHNIC AND RACIAL PATTERNS

In 1970, the Census Bureau designated four counties as the Cleveland Standard Metropolitan Statistical Area (SMSA). The SMSA encompasses Cuyahoga County, Geauga County to the southeast, Lake County to the northeast along Lake Erie, and Medina County to the southwest. Prior to 1970, only Cuyahoga and Lake counties were considered part of the Cleveland SMSA. In order to maintain a uniform statistical comparison, this analysis includes Geauga and Medina counties in all relevant pre-1970 data. For the 1990 census, the Census Bureau renamed the SMSA. In the bureau's vernacular the four-county area became termed a Primary Metropolitan Statistical Area with the acronym PMSA.

Portions of two adjacent counties could be considered part of the Cleveland SMSA if they were not separately designated. Most area residents would consider Avon, Avon Lake, Boston, Boston Heights, Hudson, Macedonia, Northfield, North Ridgeville, Richfield, Sagamore Hills and Twinsburg as part of greater Cleveland. These communities are located in either eastern Lorain County-part of the Lorain-Elyria SMSA or in northwestern Summit County-part of the Akron SMSA.

The four-county Cleveland SMSA had a 1990 population of 1,831,122, a decrease of 3.6 percent over the previous decade. Although the total SMSA saw an overall reduction in population, this decline was concentrated in Cuyahoga County which lost 5.8 percent, whereas Geauga, Lake, and Medina Counties witnessed a 4.5 percent increase in residents during the 1980's.[1] Since the late Seventies major interstate routes I-90 (2 West), I-271, and I-480, were completed in Cuyahoga County, opening eastern Lorain and northwestern Summit counties to residential growth. Thus, the reduction of population in the PMSA in 1990 maybe somewhat deceiving. Moreover, according to the U.S. Census Bureau's Population Reference Bureau, the SMSA is presently reversing past trends by gaining population. The Cleveland PMSA increased her overall population by one percent between 1989 and 1992, from 1,831,122 to 1,843,409.[2] By far the largest entity in the PMSA is the city of Cleveland. The Forest City represented 27.6 percent of the total population of the SMSA, and almost 36 percent of Cuyahoga County residents reside in the city according to the 1990 census. Cleveland remains the area's cultural, economic, political, and recreational focal point.

The ethnic and racial composition of the SMSA has changed dramatically since the founding of what was intended to become the capital of New Connecticut in 1796. Prior to the completion of New York's Erie Canal and Cleveland being designated as the terminus for the Ohio Canal, the hamlet was inhabited primarily by New England-ers of British ancestry. Many of the German and Irish immigrants lured by the canals business prospects and employment opportunities remained, enabling Cleveland to become recognized as a city (al-though she was denied the distinction of becoming Ohio's first city, by neighboring Ohio City).

Later, canal expansion and the building of the Cleveland, Columbus, and Cincinnati Railroad encouraged more diversity as Scotch, Welsh, Bohemian (Czech and Slovak), Hungarian, and Italian immigrants emigrated to Cleveland. By 1860, 44 percent of Cleveland's population was foreign born. As the city's economy diversified after the Civil War, a steady stream of immigrants flowed into the Forest City, increasing from Southern and Eastern Europe. At the turn of the century, Cleveland became the largest Slovak and Slovenian city in the world, the city also recorded the greatest concentration of Hun-garians outside of Hungary. By 1930, there were more than 36,000 foreign-born Poles in Cleveland. As the ethnic composition of the city altered, more affluent earlier immigrants began to migrate to the emerging train-and later trolley-linked suburbs.[3]

World War One prompted a third major wave of immigration into the city. Wartime production and the draft introduced unprec-edented opportunities for Southern blacks and Appalachian whites. Although many were later replaced by returning veterans, the Twen-ties kept the glint of full employment alive. The subsequent depres-sion terminated opportunities almost universally but massive govern-ment spending to meet the needs of the Second World War restored America's and Cleveland's economy.

The postwar baby boom elevated Cleveland's population to an all-time peak in 1950. Overcrowded conditions, pent-up demand caused by wartime restrictions, new industrial production techniques, and the federal government's guarantee of low interest loans to the former veterans and the building of interstate highway system all provided the impetus to move into suburban areas. Further this outward migration was accelerated when Cleveland launched the nation's largest urban renewal effort. The dislocation of thousands of poorer inner city residents precipitated a large, mostly black, influx into what had previously been predominantly ethnic areas of the city dramatically contributing to a white emigration into the surrounding suburbs. Once stability was restored, an emerging black middle class also joined the exodus into the suburbs.

During the 1940's, 1950's, and 1960's, Cleveland attracted a large number of immigrants displaced by the Second World War, the

Korean Conflict, the Hungarian Revolution and the conflicts in the Middle East. Economic uncertainty and political turmoil abroad also encouraged a diverse migration into Cleveland from Asia, the Indian Sub-Continent and from Central and South America. Cleveland's newest immigrants are typically Hispanic, Asian or American Indian. By 1990, Hispanics represented 4.6 percent of the city's population. Although three quarters of Cleveland's Hispanic community immigrated from Puerto Rico, during the 1980's and 1990's, the city began to attract a growing number of Central and South American residents. During the 1980's, the city's Asian and Native American populations increased by over 30 percent.[4] In addition, the end of the Cold War and the dissolution of the Soviet Union and Yugoslavia fostered immigration from these emerging republics to Cleveland during the early 1990's.

According to the 1990, census the largest racial groups within the city not specifically designated in tables 9 and 10 are as follows: the Pureto Ricans 17,829, Mexicans 1,991, Chinese 1,645, American Indians 1,526, Asian Indians 687, Vietnamese 672, Filipino 650, Cambodians 343, Koreans 302, and Japanese 233. Among the Clevelanders who reported an Arab ancestry, the largest numbers came from Lebanon 1,243, Palestine 407, Syria 306, and Egypt 155. The overall population changes and racial composition of the city between 1960 and 1990 are presented in table 9[5] and Cleveland's largest ancestries are indicated in table 10.

Table 9: Population and Racial Composition
City of Cleveland
1960-1990

	1960 #	1960 %	1970 #	1970 %	1980 #	1980 %	1990 #	1990 %
White	622,942	71.4	458,064	61.0	307,264	53.5	249,585	49.4
Black	250,818	28.7	287,841	38.3	251,347	43.8	235,668	46.6
Other	2,290	0.2	4,978	0.7	15,211	2.7	20,363	4.0
Total	876,050	100	750,903	100	573,822	100	505,616	100

Source: Census Bureau

Table 10: Largest Ancestries Reported *
City of Cleveland
1990 Census

German	72,040
Irish	56,154
Polish	32,480
Italian	26,678
English	20,616
Slovak	19,688
U.S. or American	14,790
Hungarian	12,038
Yugoslavian	7,538
Czech	7,205
French	6,282
Dutch	4,951
Ukrainian	4,137
Scotch-Irish	3,757
Scottich	3,577
Russian	3,310
Arab	2,979
Lithuanian	2,227
Welsh	2,132
Greek	1,736
Swedish	1,626
Romanian	1,612

* Respondents could list more than one.
 Source: Census Bureau

Although the percentage of African Americans in the city increased during the 1980's, the actual number of black Clevelanders declined by over 15,000 (note table 9). The black migration into the suburbs has typically occurred in areas bordering on the city, more specifically into those suburbs to the east and southeast of Cleveland. During the 80's, racial incidents increased markedly particularly in white ethnic neighborhoods in Cleveland and Euclid. However, such attacks declined in the late 1980's and early 1990's. Moreover, the city of Parma, previously found guilty of racial discrimination in U.S. District Court, completed plans to introduce low income housing and make the community more accessible to blacks, see table 11.

Table 11: Number of African Americans in Selected Cities Cuyahoga County 1960-1990	1960	1970	1980	1990	%Black 1990
East					
Cleveland Heights	251	1,508	14,061	20,053	37.1
East Cleveland	804	23,198	31,980	31,007	93.69
Euclid	44	296	4,548	8,763	15.97
Southeast					
Garfield Heights	193	1,789	4,977	4,687	14.77
Maple Heights	255	698	968	3,987	14.72
West and Southwest					
Lakewood	23	21	143	507	.85
Parma	132	132	314	641	.73

Source: Census Bureau

The growth and maturity of Cuyahoga County is indicated in table 12. During the 1980's, the Native American's and Asian's within the county grew rapidly compared to the 1980 census. American Indian inhabitants increased by over 35 percent, while Asians rose nearly 50 percent by 1990. Table 13 lists the largest cities in Cuyahoga County while table 14 catalogues the major racial and ethnic groups in the county.

Table 12: Population and Racial Composition
Cuyahoga County
1960-1990

	1960		1970		1980		1990	
	#	%	#	%	#	%	#	%
White	1,389,298	84.3	1,383,749	80.4	1,129,966	75.4	1,025,756	72.6
Black	255,310	15.5	328,419	19.0	341,003	22.7	350,185	24.8
Other	3,287	0.2	8,667	0.6	27,431	1.8	36,199	2.6
Total	1,647,895	100	1,720,835	100	1,498,400	100	1,412,140	100

Source: Census Bureau

Table13: Major Cities in Cuyahoga County
1990

Cleveland	505,616
Parma	87,876
Lakewood	59,718
Euclid	54,875
Strongsville	35,308
East Cleveland	33,096
Garfield Heights	31,739
Shaker Heights	30,831
Maple Heights	27,089
West Lake	27,018

Source: Census Bureau

Table 14: Largest Racial Groups
and Ancestries Reported *
Cuyahoga County
1990 Census

Black	350,185
German	308,777
Irish	195,721
Polish	136,217
Italian	130,779
English	112,964
Slovak	88,770
Hungarian	61,681
Czech	36,913
U.S.or American	35,196
Yugoslavian	31,648
Russian	29,886
French	24,559
Scottich	22,139
Puerto Rican	20,502
Scotch-Irish	16,881
Ukrainian	16,622
Dutch	15,928
Arab	12,507
Welsh	11,501
Swedish	10,315
Lithuanian	10,027
Greek	9,106
Austrian	7,630
Romanian	6,844
Asian Indian	5,102
Swiss	4,982
French Canadian	4,465
Norwegian	4,117
Chinese	4,116
Mexican	3,780
Danish	3,033
Filipino	2,957
American Indian	2,706
Finnish	2,705
West Indians, excluding Hispainic	2,338
Canadian	2,325
Subsaharan African	2,278
Japanese	1,509
Korean	1,468

* Respondents could list more than one.
Source: Census Bureau

The changes in population and racial composition evident in the SMSA are expressed in table 15. To indicate the relative size differential between Cuyahoga County and other counties that make up the SMSA, see table 16. Also for a list of the cities in Geauga, Medina and Lake, note table 17.

Table 15: Population and Racial Composition
Cleveland: SMSA/PMSA
1960-1990

	1960		1970		1980		1990	
	#	%	#	%	#	%	#	%
White	1,646,995	86.3	1,721,612	83.4	1,522,909	80.2	1,435,768	78.4
Black	258,917	13.5	332,614	16.1	345,646	18.2	355,619	19.4
Other	3,571	0.2	9,968	0.5	30,270	1.6	39,735	2.2
Total	1,909,483	100	2,064,194	100	1,898,825	100	1,831,122	100

Source: Census Bureau

Table 16: Population and Racial Composition
Geauga, Medina and Lake Counties
1990 Census

	Geauga		Medina		Lake	
	#	%	#	%	#	%
White	79,629	98.2	120,504	98.5	209,879	97.4
Black	1,056	1.3	850	.7	3,528	1.6
Other	444	0.5	1,000	0.8	2,102	1.0
Total	81,129	100	122,354	100	215,499	100

Source: Census Bureau

Table 17: Largest Cities in
Geauga, Medina and Lake Counties
1990

Geauga	Medina		Lake	
None	Brunswick	28,230	Mentor	47,358
	Medina	19,231	Eastlake	21,161
	Wadsworth	15,718	Willoughby	20,510
	Rittman	6,147	Painesville	15,699
			Willowick	15,269

Source: Census Bureau

References

[1] *1990 Census of Population*, General Population Characteristics, Ohio, Table 1, and *Cleveland, Ohio SMSA 1980*, Table 3.

[2] In August, 1975, the Budget Director of the Office of Management and Budget combined Akron, Cleveland and Lorain-Elyria into a Standard Consolidated Statistical Area to compile economic and social data. Ultimately, this became the Consolidated Metropolitan Statistical Area (CMSA) in the 1990 Census when the Census Bureau combined the Akron, Cleveland, and Lorain-Elyria SMSA's into the Cleveland-Akron CMSA. Two excellent sources for information about the CMSA are the Center for Regional Economics Issues (REI), Weatherhead School of Management, Case Western Reserve University, and the Northern Ohio Data and Information Service (NODIS), the Urban Center, College of Urban Affairs, Cleveland State University.

The CMSA also increased in population between 1989 and 1992 according to Population Reference Bureau by 1.1 percent. *Plain Dealer*, January 13, 1994 and February 8, 1994.

[3] See "Beyond Cleveland: Our Place in the Global Village" (1987) and "Beyond the Melting Pot" (1985) Cuyahoga Community College Faculty Symposiums, Thomas F. Cambell and Edward M. Miggins, contributing editors, *The Birth of Modern Cleveland 1865—1930* (1988), "A Citizen's Guide to Cleveland," League of Women Voters (1985 and 1992), William Ganson Rose, *Cleveland the Making of a City* (1990), John J. Grabowski and David D. Van Tassel, contributing editors, *The Encyclopedia of Cleveland History* (1987), *Plain Dealer*, May 3, 1991 and May 24, 1992.

[4] *1990 Census of Population*, Race and Hispanic Origin, Table 5.

[5] *1990 General Population Characteristics for the State of Ohio* and *1990 Census of Population Social and Economic Characteristics*.
Sources used for the comparative tables are the *Cleveland, Ohio SMSA 1960*, the *1960 Census of Population* to compute Geauga and Medina Counties, the *1970 SMSA*, the *1980 SMSA*, the *1990 Census of Population*, the *1990 Census of Population and Housing*, and the *1990 Census of Population and Housing Summary tape file.*

Invaluable sources for answering specific census questions are NODIS, REI, the Government Documents Department at the Cleveland Public Library, the Maple Heights and Parma Regional Branches of the Cuyahoga County Public Library system, and this book.

OHIO - CMSA's, SMSA's/PMSA's, MSA's

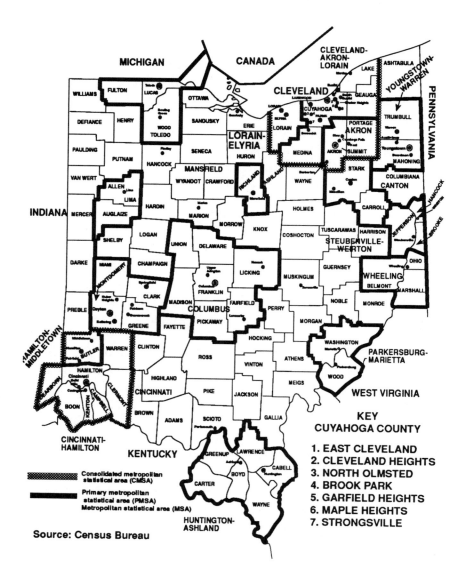

KEY
CUYAHOGA COUNTY

1. EAST CLEVELAND
2. CLEVELAND HEIGHTS
3. NORTH OLMSTED
4. BROOK PARK
5. GARFIELD HEIGHTS
6. MAPLE HEIGHTS
7. STRONGSVILLE

Consolidated metropolitan statistical area (CMSA)
Primary metropolitan statistical area (PMSA)
Metropolitan statistical area (MSA)

Source: Census Bureau

ECONOMIC AND SOCIAL CHARACTERISTICS

Typical of most major urban centers, poverty tends to be concentrated in the central city. Cleveland's poverty rate doubles that of Cuyahoga County. Eleven percent of all families in the county have incomes below the official poverty level, whereas 25.2 percent of Cleveland's households were found below this level in the 1990 census. For individuals, the pattern remained the same, with Cuyahoga County recording a 13.8 percent rate compared to the city's 28.7 percent who were found below the Federal poverty level in 1989. According to a study by the Council of Economic Opportunity of Greater Cleveland (CEOGC), by 1993, individual poverty rates exceeded 40 percent in Cleveland and increased to 19 percent in Cuyahoga County.[1] Educationally, Cleveland also lags behind the county. For example, 74 percent of the county's population over eighteen had a high school diploma and over twenty percent possessed a bachelors degree or higher, whereas in Cleveland, only 58.8 percent graduated from high school and only slightly over 8 percent recorded an education level of bachelors or higher in 1989.[2]

Cleveland's economic life represents a diversified mature industrial base. Over 43 percent of the employees in the SMSA were engaged in manufacturing in 1969, but by 1979, manufacturing positions in the SMSA declined to 30 percent of the total labor force and one fifth of all jobs in Cleveland required a college degree. According to the 1990 Census, manufacturing had declined to only 22 percent of the overall work force within the PMSA. Cleveland's massive rebuilding during the 1980's concentrated on creating information-processing jobs located outside of the areas of the city that suffered from high unemployment and increased levels of poverty. Between June of 1992 and June of 1993, the PMSA lost an additional 5,200 manufacturing jobs. Yet overall, losses were only 400, because during this same post-recessionary period, 4,800 new positions were created; however most were lower paying, suburban, service oriented jobs.[3]

Because of the diversity of the area's economy, recessions impact the SMSA/PMSA slowly and her recovery tends to be gradual. For example, when the national economy had rebounded from the recession of the early 1970's Cleveland unemployment rate increased to 7.5 percent in 1975. Similarly Cleveland recorded an unemployment rate of 13.8 percent in 1990 due to the anti-inflationary manufacturing recession of the early 1980's.[4] Blacks represent the chief victims of economic adversity, recording an unemployment rate twice that of white workers and segregated housing patterns limit employment opportunities in much of the city. Data gathered by the Population Research Center found the city to be among the most segregated in the United States; the four other culprits being Baltimore, Chicago, Detroit and Philadelphia.[5] According to the CEOGC study, the State of Ohio took 10 months to rebound from the recession of the early 1990's, while the city took 25 months.[6] Consequently Cleveland's unemployment rate increased once again as the U.S. economy officially moved out of the recession of the 1990's. See table 18.

Table 18: Comparative Unemployment Rates
January, 1991 and April 1993

	Cleveland	Cuyahoga County	SMSA/ PMSA	Ohio	Nation
Jan.,1991	9.0	5.8	5.9	7.3	7.0
Apr.,1993	12.1	6.4	6.3	6.5	6.8
Dec.,1993	10.8	5.7	5.7	6.1	7.0*

* Federal calculation - based on the 1990 census.
Source: Ohio Bureau of Employment Services

Aside from a few noteworthy developments, such as Park Centre, the Riveredge Condominiums, and Mayor White's recent initiatives, few middle and upper class residential units have been built in Cleveland since 1960. Parental fear of busing continued to prevent the city from maintaining or attracting younger families to Cleveland. The elimination of this obstacle should create a reversal of this fifteen-year dilemma. Ironically, busing continued despite the fact that many of the former segregated neighborhoods in the city became integrated. Because a large number of white parents enroll their children in parochial or private institutions, the city's school system tends to be overwhelmingly black. Mayor White's school initiatives hopefully may succeed in altering this policy.

Thus the level of maturity of the Cleveland SMSA discriminates against specific groups in the area. Cleveland residents and Africa Americans in particular are adversely affected by the increased need for skilled manufacturing and service jobs and the decline in entry level manufacturing positions. Note the disparities of wealth within the PMSA in table 19.

Table 19: Per Capita Income in 1989 by Race
Persons 15 Years and Over

	Cleveland	Cuyahoga County	SMSA/ PMSA
White	$11,161	$16,971	$16,617
Black	$ 7,369	$ 9,041	$ 9,093
American Indian, Eskimo, or Aleut	$ 9,015	$10,218	$10,780
Asian or Pacific Islander	$ 7,867	$18,601	$18,631
Other Race	$ 7,305	$ 8,023	$ 8,007

Source: 1990 Census of Population and Housing
Summary Tape File 3A

Cleveland's high poverty and unemployment rates have also contributed to an increase in teenage homicides. Although the overall murder rate declined in both Cleveland and Cuyahoga County, the number of teenage homicide victims increased steadily since 1990. According to official statistics from the Federal Bureau of Investigation in 1993, Cleveland's 22 teenage deaths represented over 14 percent of the total victims in the city and 19 percent of the county's homicide fatalities were 19 years of age or under, 42 of 221. Despite media and newspaper coverage, males, teenagers, the poor, and minorities tend to be the principal victims of crime in the United States. Teenagers are twenty times as likely as those over 65 to be the victims of a violent crime and males ages 12 through 19 are twice as likely as females to be victimized. See table 20. Similarly those whose annual income is less than $7,500 are victimized at twice the rate as those Americans whose income exceeds $50,000. See table 21. Moreover the murder rate for blacks exceeds whites by nearly 600 percent and the incidents of rape among black females are nearly three times higher than those of whites. Note table 22.

Table 20: Crime Victims: Sex and Age
Victims of Violent Crime Per 1000
United States 1990

Age	Female	Male
12 - 15	44.1	92.2
16 - 19	53.8	94.7
20 - 24	48.5	78.4
25 - 34	28.6	44.3
35 - 49	16.8	21.6
50 - 64	36.3	8.9
65 and over	3.3	3.7

Source: Bureau of Justice Statistics, 1990.

Table 21: Crime Victims: Income and Race
Victim Rate Per 1000
United States 1990

Income	White	Black
Under — $7,500	49.5	54.9
7,500 — 9,999	36.6	38.1
10,000 — 14,999	35.0	51.5
25,000 — 24,000	29.5	30.7
25,000 — 29,000	24.3	33.5
30,000 — 49,999	23.1	23.1
50,000 and over	20.7	29.1

Source: Bureau of Justice Statistics, 1988, 1990.

Table 22: Crime Victims: Race and Offense
Victim Rate Per 1000
United States 1990

	White	Black	Hispanic
Robbery	4.5	13.0	13.9
Assault	23.0	26.0	23.1
Theft	63.6	64.0	59.9
Violence	28.2	39.7	37.3

1988 Crime Rate Per 100,000

Rape	.9	2.6
Murder	5.4	31.2
Murder-Male	7.9	52.3

Source: Bureau of Justice Statistics, 1988, 1990.

Nationwide, America's response to crime has been incarceration rather than employment or rehabilitation. By 1990, 6.5 percent of all white, 10 percent of all Hispanic and 24 percent of all black males between the ages of 20 and 29 were in prison or under court control (probation or parole). According to the Ohio Department of Rehabilitation and Corrections, Cuyahoga County residents represent over 22 percent of Ohio's prison population.[7] For a list of the offenses that send the most Ohioans to prison, see table 23 and note the emphasis upon drug related offenses rather than violent crimes.

Table 23: Ohio Prison Population
Top Offenses - 1990

Theft	2,505
Drug Abuse	1,975
Aggravated Trafficking in Drugs	1,483
Trafficking in Drugs	1,228
Receiving Stolen Property	998
Breaking and Entering	971
Burglary	582
Robbery	573
Aggravated Burglary	467
Aggravated Robbery	425

Source: The Ohio Department of Rehabilitation and Correction

In a declining economy, violent crime increases. When the national murder rate increases to 9 or above per 100,000, America has entered a recessionary period. According to the Commerce Department, the U.S. economy rebounded dramatically during the final quarter of 1994, growing at a phenomenal 7.5 percent annual rate.[8] Hopefully, this is indicative of a long term trend. Note table 24.

Table 24
Murder Rates in U.S.
Homicides Per 100,000 Population
1970 - 1993

Year		Rate
1993	---	9.5
1992	---	9.3
1991	---	9.8
1990	---	9.4
1989	---	8.7
1988	---	8.4
1987	---	8.3
1986	---	8.6
1985	---	7.9
1984	---	7.9
1983	---	8.3
1982	---	9.1
1981	---	9.8
1980	---	10.2
1979	---	9.7
1978	---	9.0
1977	---	8.8
1976	---	8.8
1975	---	9.6
1974	---	9.8
1973	---	9.4
1972	---	9.0
1971	---	8.6
1970	---	7.9

Source: Federal Bureau of Investigation

Reference

[1]*Advisory Commission on Inter-government Relations*, Fredrich Stocker, "Fiscal Disparities Cleveland, Ohio Metropolitan Area," 1967, p. 250, *SMSA 1980*, and the *1990 Census of Population and Housing*, Income and Poverty Status 1989, table 9.

[2]*1990 Census of Population and Housing*, Education and Veteran Status, table 3.

[3]*County Business Patterns*, 1968, table 3, *SMSA 1960, 1960 Census of Population, SMSA 1970, SMSA 1980*, Stocker, pp. 252—254, *Plain Dealer*, May 18, 1991 and October 2, 1993.

[4]*U.S. Department of Commerce Population Report*, "Characteristics of Selected Neighborhoods in Cleveland, Ohio, April, 1965," January 23, 1967, p. 15, *SMSA 1970, U.S. News and World Report*, October 20, 1975, and the *Plain Dealer*, May 16, 1991.

[5]*Plain Dealer*, May 18,1991.

[6]*Plain Dealer*, October 2, 1993.

[7]Damaine Vonada, editor, *1992/1993 The Ohio Almanac* (1992) p. 402.

[8]*Plain Dealer*, March 2, 1994.

In Russia, economic chaos has contributed to the growth of organized criminal enterprises. Moreover, the F.B.I. and local police have discovered Russian crime groups operating in Boston, Cleveland, Chicago, Dallas, Minneapolis and New York, *U.S. News and World Report*, March 7, 1994.

CLASS STRUCTURE,
FISCAL AND POLITICAL DYNAMICS
Class Structure

Class orientation is largely based upon an individual's capability to comprehend and sacrifice for the future. This idea was originally presented by Edward C. Banfield in his *The Unheavenly City: The Nature and Future of Our Urban Crisis*. According to Banfield's analysis, the further one can project into the future, the higher his or her social class. Time rather than income represents the principal determining factor in understanding an individual's social class orientation. Social class is, therefore, more a product of perception rather than of one's monetary position.[1]

In addition, an individual's ability to delay gratification is also an indication of maturity, not reflected by longevity. Formulating the patience and perseverance to conceive of long-term goals and complementing them are elements of this maturation process. Developing a basic concern for others and the humility to admit one's errors are all examples of maturity,[2] the greater the maturation level the higher the social status.

During infancy, a child often demands instant gratification to meet biological needs representing the "id" in Freudian terminology. As a child becomes socialized by his association with others, like family members and peers, a conscious personality develops, Freud's "ego". Arbitrating between basic desires and societal values is an individual's internalized conscious, the "superego". According to Sigmund Freud and his adherents, an improperly defined superego could lead to aggressiveness, inferiority feelings, low self esteem and the inability to work well with others, in terms of class orientation, the less socialized an individual is the lower his social status, and the greater the likelihood of anti-social behavior.[3]

The classes outlined herein are not set in stone, an individual may have been groomed into one class and rebel or aspire to another as parental, educational, peer and religious values may be questioned or challenged by one's life experiences. In this analysis the upper, middle, working and lower classes are described in a pure form. Just as a child grows to adulthood, most individuals are in transition as age and knowledge confront prior beliefs and attitudes.

At the upper end of the time continuum is the upper class. Long life dominates this class to a sense of immortality, they wish to make their mark to benefit descendants for generations yet unborn. The upper class will commit their efforts and resources to enhance and protect a future for their lineage, everything from local issues to global concerns occupy their activities. Deeply committed to formal organizations and public service, the upper class believes their involvement in these entities will positively affect the future and their descendants.[4]

The upper class quickly elevates a child to adulthood, rapidly the child is given opportunities to make decisions. Therefore, the upper class child is also granted far more freedom and responsibilities than his/her counterparts; and the child is expected to expand his/her horizons while not infringing upon others:

> The upper-class individual is markedly self-respecting, self-confident, and self-sufficient. He places great value on independence, curiosity, creativity, happiness, 'developing one's potentialities to the full,' and consideration for others. In rearing his children, he stresses these values along with the idea that one should govern one's relations with others...[5]

By emphasizing creativity and independence the upper class promotes divergence. Fundamental differences are almost inevitable when one considers today's impact upon the future, for example, nuclear power could be viewed by some as a viable alternative energy source while others could perceive it as a catastrophe waiting to happen. Politically, the upper class represents the chief contributors to nearly every political philosophy imaginable from the Democrats and Republicans, to the Libertarians and Natural Law Party, to supporting candidates as diverse as John Anderson, Lyndon LaRouche, H. Ross Perot, and George Wallace.

Similarly, this encouragement of self-expression affects the upper classes attitude toward art and sex. Generally a global appreciation of artistic endeavors and toleration characterizes the upper class, this independence invites a range of appreciation which may extend from cubism to the works of Robert Mapplethorpe or Andy Warhol. Often this class accepts a liberated sexual attitude toward consensual adult relationships and in their concern for others the upper class deplores bigotry, racism, and violence. Somewhat reclusive, of all classes the upper class demand privacy.[6]

When Alexis de Tocqueville visited America in the 1830's, he found that the whole of U.S. society seems to have melted into a middle class which he found to be "economical," rather than "enlightened or generous."[7] Overwhelmingly, Americans perceive themselves as being middle class, in public opinion polls that allows for a subjective opinion on social class, respondents will indicate a decided preference for a middle class category irregardless of their income.[8]

The middle class is future oriented but not to the same extent as the upper class. They look, at times longingly, to becoming grandparents. Middle class individuals often volunteer their expertise and their time to community activities and they join organizations that usually provide for some service to those in need, like the Jaycees or the Shriners. Although they deplore bigotry, racism, and violence, they are often more willing to accept a received opinion, unlike the upper class who question all unsubstantiated statements. Far less controversial in their beliefs, the middle class generally accepts conventional attitudes toward sex, art, and politics.[9]

The immediate family dominates the life-style of the middle class, often preoccupied by their pursuit of wealth and personal gratification within the nuclear family, they are less involved in community activities or the extended family unit than the upper class. Self-centered and self-indulgent they often find solace in entertaining a like-minded circle of friends and co-workers, and avidly pursue recreational activities. Although the work place often occupies much of their time, they do vote. The middle class tends to be less concerned with privacy, and they are more focused on keeping up or moving up with their neighbors or co-workers.

Middle class children are granted the freedom to develop self-expression and independence in their formative years but once placed in an educational matrix, particularly if difficulties arise, the child is often confronted by rules and requirements. For some of the children, if the originally imposed sanctions were in fact enforced they would find themselves grounded until their 20's or 30's. Middle class parents are actively involved in the educational achievements and progress of their offspring. Since education is perceived as the vehicle for future employment, they expect their children to go to college to become successful, education having a secondary place to developing a marketable job skill as Allan Bloom aptly pointed out in *The Closing of the American Mind*.[10]

Although generally self-reliant, the working class individual is less confident that he can shape the future. The future is somewhat fated beyond his control. For example, an unsuccessful effort at obtaining a promotion would commonly be attributed to bad luck rather than any other criteria. Self-righteous, more aggressive, and less mature than the middle class, the working class tends to accept prejudicial, violent behavior. The working class will join organizations for fun. A good working class bar serves mixed drinks, a shot and a beer. Without a deeper commitment to the future or the community, they randomly participate in the election processes and normally vote along ethnic or party lines.[11]

Rules are imposed swiftly upon a working class child. During the formative years a child is raised to respect neatness, cleanliness, honesty, obedience and authority. As working class children become teenagers, the restrictions fall to the wayside as the child is expected to quickly fend for him or herself. Although removing the child from the household seems to be the main objective, the working class has a deep attachment to the family and their overall generosity to less fortunate members of the family may be unparalleled.[12]

Without the resources of the other classes, the primary objective of the lower class is survival. Endless welfare procedures, the tedium of unemployment, medical and nutritional deficiencies, and violence, plague the lower class. All of these elements seem to contribute to perpetuation of poverty and federal and state welfare policies seem designed to foster a permanent under-class in America. After the U.S. Supreme Court legalized abortions in *Roe v Wade* in 1973, Congress passed the Hyde Amendment which prohibited the use of Federal Medicaid funds for this purpose in 1976. Moreover, federal guidelines forbade using food stamps to purchase contraceptives. Until the Clinton administration mandated that states allow Medicaid to fund abortions in cases involving rape and incest, in April 1994, all forms of reproductive choice were denied to those women on Medicaid. Furthermore, in order to receive Aid for Dependent Children (ADC) in Ohio, an applicant must be unemployed and may not possess more than $1,500 in personal property. Meeting this criteria allows a parent with two children a monthly ADC stipend of $341, excluding food stamps.

Without a means of transport, food stamp recipients normally shop at small local grocery or convenient stores whose inflated prices are legendary. Often unable to stretch food budgets for an entire month, relatively inexpensive starchy foods substitute for nutrition. Although medical care is provided for those on ADC, families commonly delay attention until an emergency room visit. Although the overwhelming majority of lower class individuals are law abiding citizens aspiring to advance to a middle class life-style, they are the chief victims of crime and gang violence[13] (see tables above).

According to the Ohio Department of Human Resources, many of the perceptions about welfare are false. Seldom do ADC recipients remain on state assistance beyond two years, few have more than two children and recipients tend to be white and increasing in numbers. See table 25.

Table 25: ADC Case Load by Race
State of Ohio 1990

White	128,474
Black	75,961
Hispanic	3,479
Other	1,598
Not Given	45,175

ADC Total Recipients 1990 and 1993

1990	626,001
1993	710,622

Source: The Ohio Department of Human Resources and Cleveland Public Library Public Assistance Monthly Survey, July, 1993.

Young males raised in a matriarchal family are swiftly recruited, sometimes during puberty, into neighborhood gangs. Also, without male role models or local employment opportunities, the young may turn to criminal activities to fulfill basic economic and sexual needs and desires. Males tend to resent authority and have little attachment to their community, whereas nurtured females tend to remain in school and identify with middle and working class values.[14]

Fiscal and Political Dynamics

Cleveland is surrounded by some 60 municipalities in Cuyahoga County and over 90 in the SMSA as a whole and a total of 33 school districts operate within Cuyahoga County and 57 in the PMSA. A growing number of single function districts operate within Cuyahoga County, e.g. the Metroparks, a county library system, a Regional Sewer district, soil conservation, a nearly regionalized trash collection, regional transit, and police and fire through the county-wide adoption of a 911 emergency phone number. Although Cleveland receives revenues from suburban areas, principally through a two percent income tax and water charges from the municipal water system, her position relative to these municipalities is not one of control. Attempts at forming a metropolitan government for Cuyahoga County in 1969 and 1970 failed and any attempt by the city to extend effective authority over the metropolitan area through annexation would be improbable:

> The metropolitan area is highly fragmented into
> numerous small jurisdictions, with the result that
> there are wide disparities in tax loads and service
> levels and administrative diseconomies associated
> with small scale, often uncoordinated, operation.
> The fact that the central city of Cleveland is com-
> pletely encircled by suburban municipalities rules
> out annexation as a means of enlarging the service
> area.[15]

The relationship between the SMSA and the State of Ohio is also noteworthy. Daniel Elazar presented perhaps the best portrait of National and Ohio politics in his *American Federalism: A View From the States*. Elazar found evidence of three cultural patterns which extended throughout America, the moralists, the individualists and the traditionalists.

Throughout most of New England, the northern Midwest, and upper west to upper California, Elazar found the moralists. This northern political philosophy believes that the political process is healthy, they believe that it is a duty for all citizens to be involved in politics, they welcome new initiatives and are gener- ally supportive of their political appointees. Generally more environmentally oriented, they tend to ridicule the rest of the country for their failure to meet green (environmental) stan- dards.[16]

In a band stretching from the eastern and southern portion of the old Confederacy to southern California, are the traditional- ists. Traditionalists generally retain the original Jeffersonian Democratic belief in states rights. New initiatives are often re- sisted by the traditionalists because they threaten the status quo and any enlargement in the Federal bureaucracy is usually per- ceived as a threat to local control. They generally believed that participation in government and the political process should be a privilege reserved for prominent families whose influence once cultivated or fertilized the political scene. The traditionalists often believed that politics should be a preogative reserved to the elite.[17]

Between these two pervasive beliefs, Elazar found the individualists, a kind of money grubbing, sinister, avaricious, Ohio type politics. An individualist culture believes that elective officials seek opportunity for self-employment and other selfish motives. Bureaucracy is viewed as a possibility to feather one's own nest. Too often this mercenary view of state politics results in a knee jerk reaction — dirty politics. Cynicism abounds in individualist's states; it abounds in Ohio.[18]

According to Elazar's analysis, Ohio is primarily an individualist state, mistrustful of its political leaders. This may be partly attributed to the nature of the state's economy. Ohio is a pluralistic state producing a vast multitude of industrial and agricultural goods. Her diversity extends, in agriculture, from growing tobacco along the Ohio River to wine production along Lake Erie, and in industry, from oil production to high-tech medical equipment, inclusive of nearly everything in between. Representing these divergent elements are a vast multitude of lobbying activities by manufacturing, labor, agricultural, and consumer interests.

Another contributing factor to this somewhat cynical nature of the SMSA toward state politics was particularly evident in its lack of representation in the state legislature. Until the U.S. Supreme Court overturned the legislative apportionment of Ohio in 1967, based on the *Baker* and *Reynolds* decisions, major cities in the state were greatly under-represented. However, it should also be noted that moralistic views prevail at times in the SMSA. Elazar classified Northeastern Ohio as MI, moralist and individualist.

The election of Richard Celeste from Cuyahoga County as governor brought an infusion of unparalleled state spending into this region, restoring some confidence in state government, at least until 1990. Many of Governor Celeste's programs encouraged state-wide participation, e.g. encouraging residents and the state to buy Ohio products, touting tourism, rotating the capital throughout the state, and increasing aid to education. Politics and the economic slowdown of the early 1990's have squashed these initiatives. During the last ten years, a dozen states and communities have sought to increase revenues and promote tourism by supporting casino gambling while Ohio, the third most visited state in the nation, languishes.

As a product of the low tax philosophy of the 1960's and 1970's, the city's inability to properly maintain municipal services ultimately contributed to cooperative regional responses to common problems. For example, regional transit succeeded in upgrading and modernizing the entire county-wide commuter system while the state similarly improved the former city operated lakefront parks. Regionalization also enhanced the holdings of the zoo, constructed bike and hiking trails, completed a state-of-the art Rain Forest, and allowed for the expansion and modernization of much of Metropark system.

In the 1980's, an important and positive change resulted from the city's default. After powerful local banks refused to roll over debts, the city was forced into fiscal default. Cleveland raised the income tax to two percent to restore the monetary integrity of the city and this reduced her reliance on property taxes to finance municipal operations.

Though the economic dislocation caused by moving from a manufacturing base to service-oriented enterprises ravaged many areas, the Cleveland SMSA changed directions and began to rebound. As Clevelanders rediscovered the Cuyahoga River, boating and Lake Erie, the Flats came alive and upwardly mobile suburbanites began to return to a rehabilitated Ohio City, Cuyahoga River condominiums, loft and warehouse dwellings. Despite severe economic downturns during the recurring recessions in the 1980's and early 1990's, this area seemed to have turned a corner and this aura of optimism has continued to prevail in this region. See above, "A City Reborn."

Although the fortunes of major employers attract the greatest media attention, small business represent the backbone for American job creation. To assist local firms, the Greater Cleveland Growth Association developed the Council of Small Enterprises (COSE). COSE united 13,000 businesses into a single negotiating unit to address such shared problems as the spiraling cost of medical care. This effort served for years as a national model and undoubtedly inspired some of President Clinton's health care reform initiatives.

When Mayor Michael White promoted an active involvement of the business community in initiatives designed to address the city's major social problems, Cleveland seemed to be on the right track with all cars becoming aligned. Attesting to the cooperative effort between the mayor's office and the business community, the city witnessed the greatest home building effort since the early 1950's. Additionally, the mayor developed a close working relationship with the owners of the Cleveland Indians and the Cleveland Cavaliers, Richard Jacobs and George Gund, respectively, in resolving problems arising from building the nation's largest private and public funded venture - Gateway. In addition, Cleveland, "the Renaissance City," became the only city to be awarded the recipient of the All-American City Award for an unprecedented fourth time within a dozen years in 1993.

Mayor White's determination to stop bank redlining of selective Cleveland neighborhoods resulted in pledges by banks to end discriminatory loan practices. By January 1994, area banks made commitments in excess of a billion dollars in mortgage, small business, real estate and home-improvement loans to Cleveland neighborhoods to redress former loan disparities. Once again Cleveland paved the way for others to follow.[19]

In February, the national limelight was again focused on the city when the Greater Cleveland Growth Association chose a black female, the immensely capable Carole F. Hoover as their president. Hover had previously served as the chief liaison between the mayor's office and the business community.[20]

Probably the best example of the type of mutual cooperation that the mayor's office sought to achieve was witnessed in financing the Crittenden Court Apartments in June 1994. The funds needed to build the first new downtown apartment complex in over 20 years was secured by combining the resources of the business community, government and labor. Loans to build the Crittenden Court were obtained from AFL-CIO Housing Investment Trust, Cleveland Tomorrow, the City of Cleveland, HUD, and the Ohio Carpenters Pension Fund.[21]

Thus, the Cleveland SMSA faces issues and problems which are both unique and others which typify those encountered by other major metropolitan areas. The diverse industrial base provides some immunity to economic dislocation. Cleveland also typifies many of the same economic and social problems encountered by other urban centers: e.g. unemployment, poverty, and a disparity of wealth. Despite the loss of population in the city of Cleveland, the loss of manufacturing jobs, and the severe recessions of the 1980's and 1990's, this area witnessed an inordinate amount of construction and redevelopment. An interesting observation presents itself— these losses may have actually contributed, as a catalyst, to the corporate entities of this area to realize the vitality and potential to this community.

Among these noteworthy accomplishments were the building of the BP and TRW headquarters, the creation of the International Exposition Center (I-X Center), the expansion of the Cleveland Clinic, a state-of-the-art Cleveland Play House, the redevelopment of Playhouse Square, the expansion of the Flats, the completion of a major east-west interstate highway I-480, the Inner Harbor, Tower City, a Convocation Center for Cleveland State University, a new stadium and arena for major sports activities, the East Side Market, Church Square, the *Plain Dealer's* new Production and Distribution Center, and the building of the Rock and Roll Hall of Fame and Museum. Moreover, the SMSA witnessed an overall increase in population between 1989 and 1992. Cleveland's assets far exceed her liabilities. According to *Places*

Rated Almanac, Cleveland ranked 14th as the best place to reside among North America's 343 major cities and towns in 1994.[22]

Cleveland, Cuyahoga County, the SMSA/PMSA, and CMSA are in transition. Although manufacturing remains the basic core of greater Cleveland's economy, high-tech computer, medical, polymer and scientific research represents the most rapidly expanding portions of this areas economy, while the recreational and the service sectors offer numerically the most job-producing components for employment opportunities. Correspondingly, the more attractions that this locality possesses, the greater the likelihood that business, commercial, and investment opportunities will spill over into development and future job creation.

Increasingly, our collective economic future seems linked to tourism and every avenue should be explored to promote this area as a user-friendly vacation destination. Brochures depicting local attractions, historical sites and recreational activities should be made easily accessible for travelers to Cleveland-Hopkins. Perhaps a Cleveland Visitor and Information Center could be maintained at the airport and at other transit locations like Tower City. Everything from money exchanges and translation services for international travelers to downtown carriage rides and an operating casino should be considered to attract visitors. For example, tourist buses could easily link Cleveland's attractions to Akron's Inventor's Hall of Fame, Quaker Square and Stan Hywet Hall and Canton's Football Hall of Fame and William McKinley's homestead.

Although the Cuyahoga Valley National Recreational Area, complemented by Cuyahoga Valley Scenic Railroad, and Hale Farm and Village, attract thousands of visitors, the addition of a few elk, moose and buffalo, would only enhance the site for the prospective travelers. Furthermore, the National Park Service determined that the 87 mile Ohio and Erie Canal route from the Cleveland Flats to Zoar-New Philadelphia, was worthy of national recognition as an historic corridor thereby opening yet another avenue to promote tourism. NASA's Lewis Research Center's Visitor Information Center and the soon-to-be constructed Great Lakes Museum of Science, Environment and Technology will open the window to virtual reality. As the magnitude of the transformation that has already taken place in this area becomes apparent what emerges is a unique family oriented vacation location that can take you from a primeval past to the cutting edge of the future. With all the beauty and excitement that greater Cleveland has to offer, no wonder Moses emerged here from the wilderness.

References

[1]Edward C. Banfield, *The Unheavenly City: the Nature and the Future of Our Urban Crisis* (1966) chapter four and *The Unheavenly City Revisited* (1970) chapter three.

[2]Ann Landers, *Plain Dealer*, June 17, 1993.

[3]Larry J. Siegal, *Criminology* (1992) pp. 168-170.

[4]Banfield, *Revisited*, pp. 57-59.

[5]*Ibid.*, p. 57.

[6]*Ibid.*, pp. 57-59.

[7]Alexis de Tocqueville, *Democracy in America* (1959) pp. 209-210.

[8]Richard Centers, *The Psychology of Social Classes* (1949)   p. 77.

[9]Banfield, *Revisited*, p. 66.

[10]Allan Bloom, *The Closing of the American Mind* (1987) part one and two are excellent.

[11]Banfield, *Revisited*, pp. 60-61.

[12]*Ibid.*, p. 60.

[13]Ohio Department of Human Resources and the Cleveland Public Library.

[14]Banfield, *Revisited*, pp. 62-63.

[15]Stocker, p. 127.

[16]Norman R. Luttbeg, *Comparing the States and Communities Politics, Government, and Policy in the United States* (1992) pp. 50-52.

[17]Daniel J. Elazar, *American Federalism: A View from the States* (1972) pp. 90-92.

[18]John J. Harrigan, *Politics and Policy in States and Communities* (1991) pp. 23-27, Ira Slarkansky, *The Maligned States* (1972) pp. 40-41, and Thomas R. Dye, *Politics in States and Communities* (1994) pp. 10-13.

[19]*Plain Dealer*, January 20, 1994.

[20]*Plain Dealer*, February 9, 1994.

[21]*Plain Dealer*, June 29, 1994.

[22]*Plain Dealer*, June 5, 1994.

The *Places Related Almanac* included portions of the CMSA in tabulating data for the 1993 report. *Plain Dealer*, January 26, 1994.

For additional contemporary information about Cleveland see above "A City Reborn."

OFFICIALS OF 44 FIRMS DECIDE
DESTINY OF CITY

By Bob Modic

Executives of 44 Cleveland companies dominate the boards of most civic, educational and financial organizations here.

In these posts they help make the decisions which determine the direction in which the city will go or fail to go.

Their influence over the broad spectrum of community affairs determines:

WHAT INDUSTRIES will expand and where they will be located.

SUPPORT OR OPPOSITION of proposed city financing measures such as a city income tax, bond issues, levies, school building programs.

THE DISTRIBUTION of millions of dollars annually in foundation grants.

POLICIES and expansion plans of such institutions as colleges, hospitals, fund-raising agencies, the Chamber of Commerce and development foundations.

The men who serve on these civic groups are mostly board chairmen, presidents or vice presidents of Cleveland's biggest business and industrial firms. They serve without pay and despite their heavy business responsibilities, devote much time to their civic responsibilities.

They comprise what has come to be known in big cities as "The Establishment" of the community.

Who are they?

In the last three months Press reporters have studied the makeup of every important community group and institution in the city.

That study shows that representatives of these 44 firms make the major impact on most important decisions in the city:

TWENTY-TWO INDUSTRIAL FIRMS--Republic Steel, Midland-Ross, Standard Oil, Hanna Co., TRW, Cleveland-Cliff's, White Motor, Oglebay Norton, Pickands Mather, Ford, Reliance Electric, Triax, General Electric, Lubrizol, Eaton Yale & Towne, Warner & Swasey, Cleveland Twist Drill,

Medusa Portland Cement, National Acme, Clevite, General
Motors and Tremco.

FIVE BANKS--Cleveland Trust, Central National, National
City, Union Commerce and Society National.

FOUR DEPARTMENT STORES--May's, Halle's, Higbee's
and Sears.

FOUR LAW FIRMS--Jones, Day, Cockley & Reavis; Arter,
Hadden, Wykoff & Van Duzer; Squire, Sanders & Dempsey;
Thompson, Hine & Flory

THREE UTILITIES--Illuminating Company, East Ohio Gas
Company, Ohio Bell Telephone Company.

TWO NEWSPAPERS--*The Press* and the *Plain Dealer*.

TWO CIVIC ORGANIZATIONS--Chamber of Commerce
and University Circle Research Center.

ONE ACCOUNTING FIRM--Ernst & Ernst.

ONE RESTAURANT FIRM--Stouffer's.

The extent of the community influence of these firms is
indicated by their leading role in these organizations:

Their executives comprise 22 of the 27 board members of
the Chamber of Commerce whose "yes" or "no" votes usually are
vital to community issues.

They provide 24 of the 38 board members of the Growth
Board which helps to locate new or expanding industry in Northeast Ohio.

They serve on the boards which run Western Reserve
University (8 of 15 members), Case Tech (15 of 30 members), and
Cleveland State University (6 of 9 members). [Case and Western
Reserve merged in 1967].

In the Educational Research Council, which is developing
new classroom curricula for many suburban and religious schools
here, they make up 12 of the 18 board members. In the 75-mem-
ber Businessmen's Interracial Committee, 31 of the 41 white
businessmen are from these companies.

They serve as directors of the five major banks here--Cleveland
Trust (18 of 25 directors), (16 of 21), Central National (13 of 25),
Union Commerce (10 of 22) and Society National (9 of 22).

They comprise most of the board of the Cleveland Development Foundation (31 of 37 members) and University Circle Development Foundation (6 of 9), which are influential in urban renewal and other building programs.

Also the Cleveland Foundation (4 of 5 members of the
distribution committee) and the Associated Foundation (7 of 11
trustees), which determine the distribution of millions of dollars.

In the United Appeal, the community's biggest fund-raising drive, 10 of the 19 trustees and all five officers are from these companies.

The executives of these 44 companies also serve on the boards of Cleveland Opera Association (10 of 19 members) which sponsors the Music Hall programs here, the council on World Affairs (24 of 52 members), University Hospitals (21 of 44 members) and the Music Arts Association (19 of 56 members) which operates the Cleveland Orchestra.

In groups which have conducted recent tax studies here, they also have substantial rules--the Citizens League, 14 of 30 board members, and the Mayor's Tax Study Committee, 10 of 24 members.

The tendency to have representatives of Cleveland's business community head almost every kind of organization or institution here--in preference, for example, to educators, clergymen, doctors, public officials or other professions--is indicated by the composition of these boards:

Western Reserve University's trustees consist of 13 businessmen, one businessman's wife and one educator who is president of the university. University Hospitals' board also is largely businessmen and the wives of businessmen.

Art Museum trustees are eight businessmen, two wives of businessmen and three lawyers. The Cleveland Foundation's distribution committee consists of four businessmen and the wife of a businessman. United Appeal trustees are 14 businessmen, two wives of businessmen, a lawyer and two union officials.

Source: *Cleveland Press*, June 6, 1966.

WE'RE IN THE BLACK, BUT
STREETS STILL LEAN AND MEAN

by Tom Andrzejewski

While Mayor George V. Voinovich and company were holding orgies to appease the gods of default, complete with burnt offerings, some city neighborhoods didn't look much different yesterday morning than they did before Dec. 15, 1978.

Kinsman Rd. in Mount Pleasant still was a poor, tattered sister to its extension, Chagrin Blvd. in Shaker Heights. Union Ave. had a few more closed storefronts, and the man and woman waiting for the bus at E. 116th st. had to stand among glistening shards of broken glass.

The swings were up at Regent Park, near E. 65th St. and Morgan Ave., but the pool was closed. A young mother with three toddlers walked along Temple Ave. and disappeared into the overgrowth at the east side of the ragged- looking park. Chest-high weeds covered a vacant lot among the remaining houses across the street.

It's easy--and perhaps a cheap shot--to seek out such disgraces and conclude that default really didn't mean that much to folks in the street. Easy, perhaps cheap, but true.

City Hall--the 1987 version--might run better. The flow charts might be lean and mean, but that's also a way to describe the population and the streets.

"It was a self-inflicted wound," former Mayor Dennis J. Kucinich practically bellowed into the telephone at his office in the Warehouse District yesterday. He was talking to the New York Times, apparently interested in Voinovich's media event.

Kucinich was right. The other players in the 1978 drama probably would have agreed, although from a different perspective.

Default sucker-punched the city's ability to finance its recovery, and it was a setup.

Some of the people making decisions for the banks were prominent contributors to the recall campaign against Kucinich. They apparently had no problem approving the same notes involved in the default to an already overextended city under Mayor Ralph J. Perk, Kucinich's predecessor.

The six banks that demanded repayment of $15 million denied that sale of Cleveland Public Power, formerly the Municipal Light Plant--a competitor of the Cleveland Electric Illuminating Co.--would have averted default. But you would have had to be blind to miss the Anglo-Saxon winks.

As a staff report of a House Banking, Finance and Urban Affairs subcommittee concluded in April 1979:

> The interlocking relationship of the Cleveland Trust Co. (now AmeriTrust Corp.) and some of the other banks with much of the corporate community, and the deep animosities and political cross-currents in which some bank officers became involved, suggest the strong possibility that factors other than pure, hard-nosed credit judgments entered the picture.

Former AmeriTrust Chairman M. Brock Weir, the city's gonzo banker, led the pack. It was a classic Cleveland Establishment rally-round, complete with meetings at the Union Club to decide, down the line, destinies of a steelworker on Clark Ave. or a widow on Kinsman.

While AmeriTrust's leadership was intent on denying its own city's government $15 million in credit, it was making risky loans that eventually totaled $199 million to troubled Third World countries. In fact, the bank just posted a second-quarter loss of $60 million to build reserves for possible loan losses.

And here we thought it was farther to Caracas than to Cudell or Corlett.

Kucinich inherited a financial swamp under triple-canopy jungle. Perk--probably the worst modern mayor Cleveland has had--somehow lulled the town into thinking he was in control.

The signs of financial collapse were around as early as Perk's first term, but not many people paid attention.

In 1975, the Growth Association issued a report on Cleveland finances--and warned that the city was running out of money, had no potential for service improvements and redevelopment and had substantial fiscal deficiencies. Bankers did their mayor a favor and accented the positive--that the city could balance its books.

Meanwhile, Perk was issuing unvoted bonds and notes, and using the money for operating the city, which is like taking out a loan every week to pay your grocery bill.

The city had $32.3 million worth of unvoted bonds and notes outstanding when Perk took office in 1971; that had grown to $140 million when he left in 1977. Kucinich was left with $40 million in notes that had to be retired or refinanced in 1978--including the $15 million involved in the default.

Default helped bring down Kucinich, and didn't do much for anyone else. Except maybe Voinovich.

That's because it allows him to brag about how the trains all run on time now, without having to say where they're going.

Source: *Plain Dealer*, June 26, 1987.

CLEVELAND TOMORROW BOARD OF TRUSTEES
1992 - 1997

John A. Shields
First National
Supermarkets, Inc.

Thomas C. Sulivan, Sr.
RPM Inc.

Robert J. Tomsich
NESCO, Inc.

Martin D. Walker
M.A. Hanna Company

Farah M. Walters
University Hospitals of
Cleveland

Morry Weiss
American Greetings
Corporation

William J. Williams
The Huntington Bank

** Chairman
* Vice Chairman
Source: Cleveland Tomorrow

ORGANIZED CRIME IN CLEVELAND

JOHN SCALISH
ORGANIZED CRIME BOSS

d. May 26, 1976

MILTON ROCKMAN

Buckeye Cigarette Co.
Convicted: Las Vegas,
skimming money
Convicted/Released 1993

ANGELO LONARDO
UNDERBOSS

Convicted: 1983, drugs
Now a federal informant

ANTHONY MILANO
CONSIGLIERE

d. 1978 natural causes
"The Old One"

JAMES LICAVOLI
NILES & WARREN

aka, Jack White
Convicted: gambling
Card Shop,
Mayfield Rd.

ANTHONY DEL SANTER
YOUNGSTOWN

d. 1977,
heart attack
Continued conflict
with Pittsburgh

JOHN NARDI
TEAMSTERS 410

Nephew of
"The Old One"
d. May 17, 1977

LEO MOCERI
AKRON

Feast of the
Assumption
Dissapeared
August 22, 1975

Danny Greene
Numbers

After d.
Alex "Shondor"
Birns
Former numbers
drop off location:
the Islander,
Middleburg Hts.
d. October 6, 1977

Joseph Gallo
Gambling

Randall &
West Side
Social Clubs
Convicted: 1983

Thomas & Charles Sinito
Loan Sharking

Appliance Mart
Northfield Rd.
Convicted: 1980

Anthony Libertore
Laborers 810

Brother accused
of bombing homes
in North Royalton
and Strongsville.
Convicted
Released/Convicted
1993

Source: the author

COUNCIL REPRESENTATIVES
CLEVELAND CITY

1994 - 1998

WARD 1
Charles L. Patton Jr.

WARD 2
Karle B. Turner

WARD 3
Odelia V. Robinson

WARD 4
Kenneth L. Johnson

WARD 5
Frank Jackson

WARD 6
Kenneth C. Lumpkin

WARD 7
Fannie M. Lewis

WARD 8
Bill Patmon

WARD 9
Craig E. Willie

WARD 10
Roosevelt Coats

WARD 11
Michael D. Polensek

WARD 12
Edward W. Rybka

WARD 13
Gary Paulenske

WARD 14
Helen Knipe Smith

WARD 15
James Rokakis

WARD 16
Patrick O'Malley

WARD 17
Raymond L. Pianka

WARD 18
Jay Westbrook*

WARD 19
Dan Brady

WARD 20
Dale Miller

WARD 21
David M. McGuirk

* City Council President
Re-elected January 3, 1994

Index